OUR TOWN

AN AMERICAN PLAY

TWAYNE'S MASTERWORK STUDIES
ROBERT LECKER, GENERAL EDITOR

OUR TOWN

AN AMERICAN PLAY

DONALD HABERMAN

Twayne Publishers • Boston
A Division of G. K. Hall & Co.

Our Town
An American Play

Twayne's Masterwork Studies No. 28.

Copyright 1989 by G. K. Hall & Co.
All rights reserved.
Published by Twayne Publishers
A division of G. K. Hall & Co.
70 Lincoln Street, Boston, Massachusetts 02111

Copyediting supervised by Barbara Sutton.
Book production by John Amburg.

Typeset in 10/12 Sabon with Novarese display type
by Compset, Inc., of Beverly, Massachusetts.

Library of Congress Cataloging-in-Publication Data

Haberman, Donald C., 1933–
    Our town.

    (Twayne's masterwork studies ; no. 28)
    Bibliography: p.
    Includes index.
    1. Wilder, Thornton, 1897–1975.   Our town.
I. Title.   II. Series.
PR3545.I3450935   1989   812'.52   88-31998
ISBN 0-8057-8054-8 (alk. paper)
ISBN 0-8057-8048-3 (pbk. : alk. paper)

For Lidia, Sofia and Alice
Donne ch'avete intelletto d'amore

Contents

Note on References
and Acknowledgments

The photograph of Thornton Wilder is reproduced courtesy of The College of Wooster Archives.

Passages quoted herein from "*Our Town*—From Stage to Screen," originally published in *Theatre Arts Magazine,* November 1940, are reprinted by permission of Union Trust Company and Donald Gallup, Literary Executor for Thornton Wilder.

Acknowledgment for permission to quote from *The Journals of Thornton Wilder, 1939–1961* is made to Donald Gallup, editor, and the Yale University Press, publisher, © 1985 by Union Trust Company, New Haven, Conn.

Acknowledgment is made to the Estate of Thornton Wilder and to Harper & Row Publishers for special permission to quote from *Our Town* copyright 1938, 1957 by Thornton Wilder, published in *Three Plays* by Harper & Brothers Publishers; and from *American Characteristics* © 1979, published by Harper & Row Publishers.

I owe a longstanding debt for much of what I know about *Our Town* to Thornton Wilder and to his sister Isabel Wilder. I am grateful to Nicholas A. Salerno, Chairman of the English department, Arizona State University, for his encouragement; and to the Arizona State University Word Processing Center, especially James Dybdahl for his careful preparation of my manuscript.

I thank Donald Gallup, Literary Executor for Thornton Wilder, Susan Ritter of the Union Trust Company, and Brandt and Brandt Literary Agents, Inc.

To my wife and colleague, Lidia Wachsler Haberman, I am particularly indebted for reading the manuscript with her customary generous rigor.

All references to *Our Town* are to the text in *Three Plays* published by Harper & Brothers; citations are unaccompanied by any abbreviation. Wilder's *Journals* and *American Characteristics and Other Essays* are abbreviated *J* and *AC* in citations.

Thornton Wilder as the Stage Manager in a 1950 production at The College of Wooster.
Photograph courtesy The College of Wooster Archives.

Chronology
Thornton Wilder's Life and Works

1897   17 April, birth of Thornton Niven Wilder and a twin brother
                who does not survive in Madison, Wisconsin. Amos Parker
                Wilder and Isabella Niven Wilder, his parents, are descendents
                of settlers already established in New York and New England
                by the eighteenth century. Amos Wilder is editor and part
                owner of the *Wisconsin State Journal* in Madison. Isabella is
                more artistic and intellectual than her husband; she had been
                thwarted in her education because medicine, her goal, was
                thought improper. Thornton is their second son. Amos, who
                was to become a biblical scholar, was first; following Thorn-
                ton's birth Charlotte, who became a poet; Isabel, who wrote
                novels and became Thornton's companion and general sup-
                port; and Janet, who for a brief period before her marriage
                was a zoologist, were born.

1906   Family goes to China, where Amos Wilder is Consul General,
                first at Hong Kong and then at Shanghai. Thornton attends a
                German school until his mother takes the children to Berkeley,
                California, where he attends public schools.

1911–1912   Lives in Shanghai and attends the China Inland Mission
                School, Chefoo.

1912–1913   Attends Thacher School, Ojai, California.

1913–1915   Attends Berkeley High School, graduating in 1915.

1915–1917   Attends Oberlin College, which had been selected by his fa-
                ther, and where he is very happy. Writes short plays, some of
                which will appear in *The Angel That Troubled the Waters*.

1917   Enters Yale, again his father's decision. Robert Hutchins, a
                lifelong friend who would become president of the University
                of Chicago, also transfers from Oberlin to Yale. Meets Henry
                Luce and Stephen Vincent Benét. Publishes short plays and the
                four-act play *The Trumpet Shall Sound* in the *Yale Lit.*

1918–1919   Leaves Yale to serve in the U.S. Coast Guard Artillery Corps.

1919–1920	Returns to Yale and receives B. A. Sails for Europe.
1920–1921	Resident at the American Academy in Rome. Follows courses in archaeology, though he is not enrolled. Begins his first novel, *The Cabala*. Sees Luigi Pirandello's *Six Characters in Search of an Author*.
1921	Returns to United States to teach French at Lawrenceville School, New Jersey. Lawrenceville serves partly as model for Grover's Corners.
1924	First nonschool publications: "Three Sentences" (from *The Cabala*) in the *Plain Dealer* and "A Diary: First and Last Entry" in *S4N*. Takes leave of absence from Lawrenceville and begins graduate study in French at Princeton. Spends first of many summers at the MacDowell Colony, Peterborough, New Hampshire, which serves as one of the many models for Grover's Corners.
1925–1926	M.A. at Princeton. Returns to Europe. *The Cabala* is published in April 1926, and *The Trumpet Shall Sound* opens in December, directed by Richard Boleslavsky of the American Laboratory Theatre.
1927	The Wilders, who had been living in Mt. Carmel, Connecticut, move to New Haven. Amos Wilder, the father, works on the New Haven *Journal-Courier*. Thornton returns to teach at Lawrenceville. *The Bridge of San Luis Rey* is published in November. Meets Gene Tunney, the boxing champion, and Jed Harris, the stage director, during Christmas vacation.
1928	*The Bridge of San Luis Rey* is awarded the Pulitzer Prize. Meets George Bernard Shaw while traveling with Tunney in Europe. His sister Isabel joins him for a round of continental theatergoing. *The Angel That Troubled the Waters* is published.
1929	First of many lecture tours.
1930	*The Woman of Andros* is published. Goes to University of Chicago as lecturer in comparative literature, invited by his friend Robert Hutchins, president, teaching there half of each year until 1936. Savage Michael Gold review of *The Woman of Andros* in the *New Republic*. Though Wilder never answered Gold directly, he turns his attention to American subject matter.
1932	*The Long Christmas Dinner and Other Plays* published. Translates André Obey's *Le Viol de Lucrèce* as *Lucrece*, produced in New York City by Guthrie McClintic. It is a failure.

1933	*Lucrece* published. Wilder goes to Hollywood for the first time.
1934	In Chicago meets Gertrude Stein, who becomes one of his closest friends and intellectual companions.
1935	*Heaven's My Destination,* Wilder's first "American" novel, is published.
1936	Father dies. Resigns from the University of Chicago. Returns to Europe where he visits Gertrude Stein; they plan to write a novel together, but she finally writes it alone.
1937	His adaptation of an acting version of Henrik Ibsen's *A Doll's House* is produced by Jed Harris and stars Ruth Gordon, who becomes Wilder's friend and confidante.
1938	*Our Town* opens 22 January in Princeton, then Boston, then New York City. It is awarded the Pulitzer Prize. *The Merchant of Yonkers,* directed by Max Reinhardt, opens in Boston.
1939	Filming by Sol Lesser of *Our Town* begins.
1940	Film of *Our Town* opens in Boston.
1941	Travels to South America for the U.S. State Department, where he finally visits Peru, the setting for *The Bridge of San Luis Rey.* Essay on James Joyce, whose *Finnegans Wake* Wilder had been reading closely, published in *Poetry.* He returns to the University of Chicago to teach two semesters.
1942	In Hollywood writes the screenplay for *Shadow of a Doubt* for Alfred Hitchcock. Enlists in the U.S. Air Force Intelligence Corps; eventually sent to the African and Italian theaters of war and is discharged at the end of the war as lieutenant-colonel. *The Skin of Our Teeth* opens in New Haven on 15 October and in New York City in November. The play provokes a controversy about its debt to James Joyce's *Finnegans Wake.* It receives the Pulitzer Prize.
1946	Mother dies. Gertrude Stein dies.
1948	*The Ides of March* is published. He begins *The Emporium,* which he never finishes.
1949	Lectures at the Goethe Institute at Aspen, Colorado.
1950–1951	Delivers the Charles Eliot Norton lectures at Harvard on the American characteristics of classic American literature.
1951	Awarded honorary doctorates by Harvard and Northwestern.
1952	Awarded Gold Medal for Fiction by the American Academy of Arts and Letters.

1

Historical Context

It may only be a matter of perception, because we who are living in it see it so close up, but the twentieth century appears to be a particularly violent time. Two world wars and uncountable "little" wars create a scene of one big war running almost constantly, sometimes with more, sometimes with fewer combatants. Civilians in large numbers have suffered directly from military aggression. Entire cities are destroyed in minutes. Civilian populations have moved from one country to another, from one continent to another. Political changes, often connected to the wars, have been dramatic as nations struggle to create workable systems between the two extremes of democracy and totalitarianism. The economic situation, almost always part of the political and military developments, is marked by periods of absurd inflation, depression, and revolution. Culturally, "high art" and the popular arts seem to grow further apart. There are extreme disagreements within both of these general groupings, and neither of them seems able to command general respect and affection. Religious activity is taken over by the conflict between those who proclaim that "God is dead" on the one hand and the fundamentalist faithful of the various religions on the other. Over all hangs the threat of major destruction, at least, if not total annihilation, by rampant industrialization or the bomb, whichever comes first. These are very broad generalizations, with the weaknesses as well as the usefulness of such. Most of the time no one lives in generalizations, though from time to time we respond to this one or that with some kind of action.

Like most of us, Thornton Wilder in his life responded to the events around him. He was in uniform in both world wars. He believed in democracy enough to fight for it when his age and position would have allowed him to remain safely at home. He also believed in democracy enough to think that it was possible to create a serious art, with meaning, that would also be popular. The religious life was for him the only genuine life, but he was suspicious of all organized religions, dogmas, and sects. He commented about the death of God that after all it had been a dreadful God. The injustice around him intruded on his life. He quietly contributed his own time and cash (almost always a good test of commitment) to both individuals and causes.

In his writing Wilder's response was somewhat less directly involved. His position was distanced both in time and place. He tried to see events as part of some larger, and probably unknowable, sequence. But Olympian calm was not his manner. Thornton Wilder was passionately enthusiastic about the life around him, and he examined it in as much detail as possible. Rejecting any causes, cures, or explanations as final, Wilder tried to keep his attention directed toward what was enduring. He accepted the ordinariness of ideas, and the difficulty, he saw, was trying to hold several of them in mind at the same time. He was totally committed to the idea of American literature, convinced that it was different from the writing of the past. At the same time he maintained a view of a world literature that could include the masterpieces of the past beside the new American literature. So, Goethe, for example, can be regarded as sharing attitudes with Walt Whitman, apart from their profound and fundamental differences in culture, time, and place.

By the time Wilder wrote *Our Town,* he was already a successful novelist. His first novel, *The Cabala,* appeared in 1926. The following year *The Bridge of San Luis Rey* was published to extraordinary acclaim. It has sold in the millions; it has been translated into twenty languages; it turned its astounded author into a celebrity and introduced him to the world, literary and otherwise; it won a Pulitzer Prize. Wilder was never to have quite this immediate success again, though *Our Town* more slowly has gained an enduring place in American dramatic literature, and it, too, was a Pulitzer Prize winner. Still later, Wilder's *The Matchmaker,* after its initial failure, reached perhaps an even wider audience in the form of *Hello, Dolly!*.

Two other novels were published in the thirties, *The Woman of Andros* and *Heaven's My Destination*. *The Woman of Andros,* though reasonably respectfully received, provoked a controversy about its relevance to the economically underprivileged in the United States of the thirties. Michael Gold, the Marxist critic, asked about the novel, "And is this the style with which to express America? Is this the speech of a pioneer continent? . . . Where are the modern streets of New York, Chicago and New Orleans? . . . Where are the child slaves of the beet fields?"[1] Other critics and writers did not join in to form a chorus behind Gold, but no one was eager to defend Wilder either. It was all very embarrassing, and somehow Wilder was faulted.

At the same time Wilder was making a place for himself as a novelist, he was also writing plays. His play writing, in fact, had begun even earlier. From his childhood he wished mightily to become a writer for the stage. At the very time that the great success of *The Bridge of San Luis Rey* was gathering momentum, he met Jed Harris, an extremely successful New York producer and director, on the train returning from a vacation in Florida, and promised to give Harris a first look when he wrote a play. Wilder kept that promise ten years later when he showed Harris the script for *Our Town*.

Wilder's sister, Isabel, recalls that Thornton as a child had corralled his brother and sisters into draping themselves in cheesecloth and performing in his plays. As an adolescent, Wilder confessed in his foreword to his three-minute plays, *The Angel That Troubled the Waters and Other Plays,* he drew up lists of titles for plays he planned to write, and, in fact, over some fifteen or more years he did actually write forty such plays to go with the titles.

The Trumpet Shall Sound was Wilder's first full-length play. Published in four issues of the *Yale Literary Magazine,* it was produced off-Broadway in 1926 by the American Laboratory Theatre, where it ran in repertory for several months. The most enduring result of this production was Wilder's meeting Richard Boleslavsky, whose ideas about acting affected *Our Town*.

The twenties was a time of growing up for the American theater. Where previously the emphasis had been on shows and entertainments, the exuberant postwar theater greeted the arrival of Eugene O'Neill, Elmer Rice, and Philip Barry, to name only a few serious new playwrights. Economic disaster at the end of the decade brought the Great Depression and the rise of fascism in the early thirties. The response in the arts was radical, sometimes leftist; at the very least a concern for political, economic, and social forces. The focus of interest in the individual was the role these forces played in his psychological makeup. Realism became the dominant style. The critical voice of Michael Gold and his fellows was the loudest. The Group Theatre and the Federal Theatre Project appear from the perspective of fifty years to dominate the American stage of the thirties.

The thirties was a time when many rushed to subscribe to one utopian answer or another. Wilder stood apart from all these developments. He had always regarded panaceas and utopian solutions to life's difficulties, first, as irrelevant when the difficulties change, as they inevitably do, and second, as expressions of impatience with life itself. He also felt that it was impossible for him to write a play with a realistic setting.

The activity on the European stage attracted him, too, and it did not address itself directly to the social unrest in the United States. He had seen and been taken with Luigi Pirandello's *Six Characters in Search of an Author.* Jean Cocteau and André Obey especially offered models of highly theatrical stage-craft. Wilder and his sister Isabel enjoyed a play-going marathon in Germany in 1928, when they saw several of the new expressionist plays. He adapted some translations of European plays, and he translated Obey's *Le Viol de Lucrèce* (The rape of Lucretia) under the title *Lucrece.*

But Wilder was also writing *American* plays. Three of those in *The Long Christmas Dinner and Other Plays in One Act* (1931) are successful on their own, and they demonstrate the results of Wilder's testing of stage techniques that are essential to the meaning of *Our Town:* the Stage Manager, the bare stage, interrupted action, and pantomime, as well as the middle-class family and its continuity through repeated births and deaths, the sorrowful regret of the dead for life, the location of the action in vast time and space, the central figure of the woman/mother.

Still, *Our Town* in its staging and its story is an unusual play in the context of its own time. Wilder turned to the example of Jane Austen (among others) for intellectual and artistic support to justify his limited selection of materials, his neglect of events of the day, and his refusal to submit his writing to any effort to correct error. Her care with the small implied, he thought, an understanding of the large. *Our Town* makes a respectable showing in comprehensive anthologies of modern drama, but it does not lend itself to being a typical example of anything. When Harold Clurman selected *Famous American Plays of the 1930s,* he did not find room for it. Perhaps the rights to reprint were not financially practical or even available. But when he mentions it in his introduction, he suggests that it, among other good plays, was not easily representative.

Our Town is Wilder's best play. *The Merchant of Yonkers* in its revision *The Matchmaker* and the *Skin of Our Teeth* are good plays, as good in their own ways as *Our Town*. They just come after *Our Town*. Wilder worked for years on *The Alcestiad,* and he saw it performed. He apparently was not entirely satisfied with it because he did not want it published in English. He never completed the play usually called *The Emporium,* though what we have is promising, and he never completed *The Martians,* either.

Robert Ardrey recounts that at the first meeting of a class Wilder taught in creative writing, when he asked for a show of hands from the students for the form of writing that appealed most, Wilder lifted his own hand along with those of his students who wanted to write plays. This was in 1930, and Wilder was already a Pulitzer Prize winner for the novel. Eight years later Wilder fulfilled the desire represented by his raised hand, and won another Pulitzer Prize, this time for drama.

2

The Importance of the Work

Our Town has a unique problem for a play: it is performed too often. It is easy to put on. It requires no scenery and nothing out of the way for costumes. For school production, especially, it has the attraction of a big cast; every student who wants a part can get one. Almost every American has seen a school performance, and the few who have not have probably formed an opinion about *Our Town* from bad reports of school performances. Not only is it exceedingly familiar, but the familiarity exists primarily as a memory of a far less than ideal production. Everybody thinks he knows *Our Town,* and what he knows is that the play is for kids. It has become almost impossible truly to see the play free from preconceptions. This book then has two main aims: to recover the play's intellectual respectability and to demonstrate how solid and at the same time how revolutionary its stagecraft is.

Our Town is not a philosophical drama in the sense that it presents in dialogue form the explanation, discussion, or development of a metaphysics. Wilder does have ideas, but they appear in the way the characters are presented, in the stage image. Wilder's experience and his philosophical thinking are transformed to a large degree by his imagination. There is no easy dilemma to be solved. The picture itself of American living is Wilder's idea. He is in the tradition of Walt Whitman. He is a defender and explainer of American idealism. Anyone who is interested in "the way we were: in our growing up and in our marrying and in our living and in our dying" (32) will find plenty to reckon with. The way the American thinks about his living and his world are Wilder's subject.

The important areas for Wilder's consideration in *Our Town* are our "religious thinking, . . . our daily life, and . . . our assumption about the life of the family" (*AC*, 70). Just about everybody is aware somehow that *Our Town* in dramatic technique is different from other plays. The theatrical manner of *Our Town* is its meaning. It is impossible to consider what the play says from the way it says it.

Wilder, speaking about *Culture in a Democracy*, said,

> Culture in a democracy has its dangers, but it has also this hope and this promise. It has a vast new subject to write about, to think about, to express, to explore: the Man with Raised Head. . . .
>
> Democracy has a large task: to find new imagery, new metaphors, and new myths to describe the new dignity into which man has entered.
>
> (*AC*, 73)

Wilder's hope was to participate in this large task of finding new ways to express what he considered to be a new subject: "the potentialities . . . of the average man existing in a democracy" (*AC*, 69). His democratic culture is not only *about* the "Man with Raised Head"; it is also *for* him. *Our Town* is one of those rare modern works that is both meaningful and for everybody.

3

Critical Reception

Our Town has probably been seen by more people than any other American play. Popularity is not an indication of its value, of course, just of its appeal and its accessibility. Its success was not immediate at its first performances. It was not just that many people failed to appreciate *Our Town;* in the beginning almost nobody seemed to like it.

The audiences at the first performances at Princeton in January 1938 did not respond. The notices were disappointing; *Variety,* the show business trade paper, thought the show was a waste of the talents of its actors and director. When the play moved to Boston, the situation worsened. The wife of the governor of Massachusetts walked out during the performance, and she was followed by those either currying favor or simply not enjoying the play. Boston reviews were very discouraging. There was even some chance the play would close before opening in New York.

But in New York the opening night performance was greeted by a cheering audience. Brooks Atkinson, the reviewer for the *New York Times,* led the enthusiastic notices. He called the play "beautifully evocative" and "hauntingly beautiful." He acknowledged that the play's form was strange, but he said admiringly that it "escaped from the formal barrier of the modern theatre into the quintessence of acting, thought and speculation."[2] Joseph Wood Krutch in the *Nation* also noted the unusual staging; the "dramatic method," he said, "is everywhere unconventional in the extreme." He had some difficulty explaining to his readers exactly what the mood of *Our Town* was: "neither sentimental nor satiric," "hard to define," it was one of "quiet contemplation."[3]

But not everybody who went to see the play was so positive. Some were disappointed at the absence of scenery and other kinds of production glamour. Some, like Eleanor Roosevelt, thought that the play was too depressing. She said that it had "moved her and depressed her beyond words. *Our Town* . . . is . . . interesting and original and I am glad I saw it, but I did not have a pleasant evening."[4]

More seriously, Stark Young in the *New Republic* thought the play was essentially literary and not dramatic. He reported that the scene with the dead in act 3 was "a stage image that is unforgettable." And that each vignette was "perfect in its length" and "beautiful and poignant." But he also wrote that the pantomiming was the worst he had ever seen. The play's future, if it had one, was essentially as literature, and even as such it lacked the power of Sherwood Anderson's *Winesburg, Ohio* and Edgar Lee Masters's *Spoon River Anthology* to evoke small-town life.[5]

Mary McCarthy expressed for many the recognition that *Our Town* could not be easily dismissed though it did not fulfill the general expectation for art at that time. She saw the play as "essentially lyric, not dramatic," and its themes as, the "tragic velocity of life, the elusive nature of experience, which can never be stopped or even truly felt."[6] Later she recalled, "How uneasy I felt when I decided that I *liked* Thornton Wilder's *Our Town*. Could this mean that there was something the matter with me? Was I starting to sell out? Such haunting fears, like the fear of impotence in men, were common in the avant garde in those days."[7]

The New York Drama Critics Circle Prize that year was awarded not to Wilder, but to John Steinbeck for his dramatization of his novel *Of Mice and Men*. When it was revived most recently in New York City, the general view was that, although it was well-enough performed, *Of Mice and Men* was dated and had little interest. This dismissal of Steinbeck's play is probably as unjust as the early overestimation of it. But *Our Town* did win the Pulitzer Prize, which provided some relief for Wilder from the disappointment at being passed over by the Drama Critics Circle.

John Gassner, who voted for Steinbeck, has written since with sympathy and appreciation about *Our Town*. "The theatricalist form of *Our Town* enables the author to build the kind of play he wants to give us—an informal, intimate, and compellingly human drama. It is a work of tone and of wisdom."[8]

Willa Cather, the American novelist, wrote to Wilder about Americans living abroad weeping with homesickness when they read the play, and she thought he had done nothing else so fine.[9] Lillian Gish, the actress, felt it was "the greatest play of our century."[10] Raymond Massey, who played the Stage Manager in USO performances during World War II, remembered the faces of the GIs in the audiences: "The tense, rapt, even desperate looks. Some were wiping tears from their eyes."[11]

Wilder himself staged *Our Town* during the final months of the war in Europe at Caserta, Italy, where it was not a success, probably because most of the audience was made up of British troops. The postwar revival directed by Jed Harris in London was a failure, too. The play has never had much appeal for the British audience. A more surprising reception was given a production in Yugoslavia during the war. Marshal Tito wanted *Our Town* translated into Serbo-Croatian and performed as part of the celebration to mark the liberation by his partisans of Belgrade. It was arranged for Wilder to go from Italy to Yugoslavia to see the partisan actors in his play create a "smashing success."

After the United States, Germany has always expressed the greatest interest in and appreciation of Wilder. The German-language playwrights Bertholt Brecht, Max Frisch, and Friederich Duerrenmatt have acknowledged a debt to his work. Immediately after the war, productions of *The Skin of Our Teeth* and *Our Town* appeared in bombed-out Germany's theaters. A Berlin production of *Our Town* was thought to be dangerous by the Russians, who closed it down. More fuss was made for Wilder's sixtieth birthday in Germany than in the United States. The celebrations of homage at Bonn included a student performance of *Our Town*. German critical scholarship is almost entirely favorable. Many books and dissertations have been published, both general surveys of Wilder's career and studies of some particular, narrow interest, such as Claus Clüver's *Thornton Wilder and André Obey*. Most of the German critics, while respectful of *Our Town*, prefer *The Skin of Our Teeth* and *The Alcestiad*. Helmut Papajewski thought the dramatic technique was limited. "This is especially the case when behind the dramatic anthropology and the concept of archetypes there stands a metaphysic that is modest and reserved in its answers and, at least in the field of cognition, gives no more than its exponents could often declare on the basis of rational reflection."[12] Even allowing for the possibility of awkward translation, this kind of criticism seems inappropriate in tone and vocabulary for *Our Town*.

Wilder was both delighted and amused by the German adulation. He knew the German weakness for profundity and inflated solemnity. He once suggested that a suitable epitaph for his tombstone could read, "Here lies one who tried to be obliging." "The Germans heard of this and got it all mixed up, made it grandiose, and, to my horror, translated it, 'Here lies one who tried to help mankind.'"[13]

Rex Burbank's *Thornton Wilder* was the first book-length study. He places *Our Town* in the theatricalist tradition and concludes, "The life it celebrates is the simplest and least pretentious imaginable . . . yet . . . it has the depth and complexity and richness of a genuine tragic vision."[14] And Malcolm Goldstein in *The Art of Thornton Wilder* agrees: "That the play is a tragedy, despite the simplicity of the dialogue, is beyond dispute, for we see the death of Emily cutting short the happiness which the young protagonists had earned by the conduct of their lives."[15]

Francis Fergusson in what is one of the best examinations of Wilder's knowing art, "Three Allegorists: Brecht, Wilder, and Eliot," emphasizes Wilder's skill as a theater technician. "Wilder occupies a unique position, between the great books and Parisian sophistication one way, and the entertainment industry the other way. . . . The attempt which I have been making, to take him seriously as an allegorizing moralist, may be much too solemn. His plays belong to the theater; they have their proper life only there."[16]

Robert W. Corrigan described the practical consequences of Wilder's innovative theatrical techniques. "These techniques have made it possible for his plays to communicate to audiences all over the world—and for this reason in most European countries, his work is considered the most representative and significant product of the modern American theater."[17]

A Reading

4

The Daily Life

Reading a play is a peculiar activity. Plays are intended for performance, and most people naturally prefer to see them acted. If the play to be read does not have beautiful speeches, in the manner of Shakespeare, for example, or articulated ideas, in the manner of Goethe's *Faust,* the rewards of reading can seem very small. It takes practice to bring a play alive in the imagination—some never learn to do it—and a book like this one can be an aid in pointing to some of the effects that might otherwise become clear only in performance. Plays are often literature as well as texts for performance, and they deserve the same scrutiny accorded other kinds of literature because they can yield the same rewards.

I have chosen the subtitle, *An American Play,* for this book, first, because it is one of the best plays written by an American and is thought by many throughout the world to be quintessentially the American play. Second, and even more important, the subject of the play is Being an American. Wilder dramatized what he saw, and what he saw was how Americans think of themselves and their relationships to experience. How Americans live. His theme, different from his subject, and it is a thread in all his work, is: how mankind confronts overwhelming disaster. The disaster in some of his work is a physical one; the Ice Age in *The Skin of Our Teeth,* for example. In *Our Town* it is more general and more abstract, but it is the source of the dramatic conflict. Death is part of it, but death is not the disaster. Death is the event that brings awareness of the disaster.

Wilder wrote in his *Journals*, ". . . *The world has no meaning save that which our consciousness confers upon it.*" The disaster is inner, the possibility that man's consciousness will fail to project meaning onto the physical world. And by mankind, Wilder wrote, "I mean not a collective human consciousness, but that of each separate existing mind." Wilder does not wish to consider the comforts or meaning offered by organized group institutions—religion, for example. Further, he believed that not just superior consciousness, but ordinary consciousness, too, possessed the power to bring the world into existence, though it, "harassed, bound by fear in self-consciousness, brings its world into being in fits and starts, living largely in the memory of the few brief occasions when the world was thus invoked" (*J*, 200).

One of the "vehicles for this operation of bringing the world into existence" is art. *Our Town* is intended to be such a vehicle, showing Emily, in particular, as she gives meaning to the objects that surround her life, and at the same time provoking the audience into an awareness of their own living.

Gertrude Stein and her writing were overwhelmingly important in focusing Wilder's attention on the American. She was his most intimate and influential intellectual companion. At the end of 1934 Stein had visited Chicago, while Wilder was lecturing at the University of Chicago, and she returned during the winter of 1935 for a series of lectures for students selected by Wilder. These lectures were published under the title *Narration* by the University of Chicago with an introduction by Wilder. He wrote introductions to two other Stein books, *Four in America* and *The Geographical History of America*. Stein and Alice B. Toklas stayed in Wilder's apartment in Chicago, and he visited them in France that summer. Their friendship was part personal and part intellectual. Wilder fantasized that they would take a house together in Washington Square in New York City. For her part Stein planned for them to collaborate on a book; he would contribute the dialogue, she, the theme and structure. In spite of the enthusiastic seriousness of each, nothing came of these dreams, though Stein did write her novel, *Ida*. And the essays Wilder wrote for Stein's books do offer some notion of what in her ideas was so useful to Wilder: her views of human psychology, the American landscape, time, religion, language, and death. She helped him free himself, as he acknowledged, from the literal nineteenth century to live in the twentieth and write a play about it. And she made him aware of being American. He wrote to her, "Yes, I'm crazy about America. And you did that to me, too."[18]

But the tradition that Wilder sought to be part of is not only American. He loved, to use the term with Stein's meaning, *masterpieces* where he found them. Masterpieces were those works, European and Asian, as well as American, that invested with meaning the outside world apart from time, identity, and memory.

Any consideration of Wilder immediately confronts his literary enthusiasms. He wrote in his *Journals* that "It has always been quite clear to me that . . . [*Our Town* and *The Skin of Our Teeth*] were *calqués*." He made a notation on his use of the French word *calqués*, distinguishing between the dictionary meaning, slavishly copied, and what he intended: "I mean merely superimposed upon a variety of molds and prior achievements in theatrical art." He added, "The indebtedness was one of admiration and love—which is seldom the case in such borrowings" (*J*, 326). He wrote also that few recognized his "borrowings" either because of ignorance or their variety and disparateness. For these same reasons, I felt it was necessary in my reading of *Our Town* to present some of Wilder's sources, not so much to trace plot or philosophy as to provide a context for his thinking and feeling, to show the writers who prompted his response.

"'Culture,'" Wilder wrote, "is in me a second nature" (*J*, 332). To understand Wilder's nature, some knowledge of what he read and loved is helpful. Important among these writers in addition to Gertrude Stein are Dante, Goethe, George Bernard Shaw, Alfred Jarry, and Richard Boleslavsky.

My aim in organizing has been to consider the play's ideas and its dramatic techniques at the same time, since I feel they are scarcely separable. Chapters 4, 5, and 6 are determined by the play's three acts; chapter 7 considers some aspects of its appearance in actual performances.

When the audience arrives at the theater for the performance of *Our Town*, it "sees an empty stage in half-light," "No curtain. No scenery" (5). In 1938 this bare stage was an unexpected and disagreeable surprise for the audience. Artistic, even experimental sets had been in use since the twenties, but a perfectly bare stage, without even curtains, a cyclorama, or some flats to conceal the rear wall of the building—and with the stage curtain already up—was definitely unusual and disappointing. The surprise that greeted those first audiences cannot be maintained or recaptured. Most theatergoers now know about and expect the bare stage and ladders at a performance of *Our Town*. The American theater has assimilated the success of experimental theater, of off-Broadway and off-off-Broadway, which started in the fifties, though the bareness of many of these productions today is the result of economic necessity, not aesthetic conviction. Wilder from the start understood that the shock could not be maintained. "This advantage would no longer be mine twenty years from now when the theatre will be offering a great many plays against freer décors; the audiences will be accustomed to such liberties." He added parenthetically, "My play will be just as valid then, but what it has lost in surprise will be replaced by its prestige" (*J*, 22). By "prestige" Wilder did not mean anything so foolish as an illusory appearance or reputation based on something like being the first one to do it. The "prestige" of the empty stage is its authority; the audience would know "what it's all about" (*J*, 22).

In a preface written for the publication of *Our Town* but not printed Wilder remembered that since seeing some classical archaeological sites in and around Rome, where he spent 1920–21 at the American Academy, he often looked at the world around him through the eyes of an archaeologist a thousand years in the future. He repeated this observation some fifteen years later in a talk he gave before the James Joyce Society, saying that his having become aware of the view of the archaeologist altered his attitude toward life. Knowing that millions have already lived and died and that probably millions more will live and die paradoxically both reduces the importance of the individual life and makes more urgent the need to provide some validity for the reality of the unique experience. It is the *relationship* between the one, the "I," and the many that is the great concern of *Our Town*. Wilder posed the theme in a question: "What is the relation between the countless 'unimportant' details of our daily life, on the one hand, and the great perspectives of time, social history, and current religious ideas, on the other?" (*AC*, 100–1). One of the many ways Wilder answered his own question in *Our Town* was through the bare stage.

In the essay with which Wilder prefaced the volume of three plays, *Our Town, The Skin of Our Teeth,* and *The Matchmaker,* he considered the issue of the one and the many in the light of his own theatergoing. During the late twenties and early thirties he found himself admiring what he saw on the stage but having difficulty "believing" it. By belief Wilder meant some sort of imaginative recognition of its validity. He concluded that the all-but-universal box-set and its variations stifled his imagination.

The realistic box-set is one of the stylistic achievements of the nineteenth-century theater, and it was made physically possible largely as a result of, first, gas and then, electric illumination. Most typically it presents a realistic room with the fourth wall removed, or if the scene is outdoors, a kind of landscape or genre painting with the proscenium arch as the frame. The audience looks on the set as a realistic representation of a particular place. The emphasis is on the exact.

Wilder concluded that realism in the theater had degenerated to telling what William James, the American philosopher, called the "abject truth," the truth reduced to a heap of specific facts. This kind of truth was "soothing" to the nineteenth-century audience that demanded comfort, both physical and intellectual. Wilder wrote: "They loaded the stage with specific objects, because every concrete object on the stage fixes and narrows the action to one moment in time and place. . . . When you emphasize *place* in the theater, you drag down and limit and harness time to it. You thrust the action back into past time, whereas it is precisely the glory of the stage that it is always 'now' there" (*AC*, 108).

Shakespeare's Juliet in a realistic production is distanced from the audience by her particularity. "If Juliet is represented as a girl 'very like Juliet' . . . moving about in a 'real' house with marble staircases, rugs, lamps, and furniture, the impression is irresistibly conveyed that these events happened to this one girl, in one place, at one moment in time" (*AC*, 124). The audience watching such a Juliet can be comforted by the feeling that what is happening to her could only happen to her. Her uniqueness prevents any possibility of seeing *my* daughter, or even *myself* in Juliet. She is an isolated, perhaps even clinical case. The Russian playwright Anton Chekhov, a master of the realist theater, who often complained about the excessive realistic detail imposed on his plays by the actor-director Constantin Stanislavsky, is said to have described the typical member of the nineteenth-century audience as a rich woman who could weep at the sentimental and melodramatic plight of Camille, coughing to her death from tuberculosis, but who could not even imagine any sympathy for her own coachman freezing in the rain outside the theater, possibly contracting pneumonia and dying. The tears for Camille cost nothing and were a pleasure; acknowledging the suffering humanity of a coachman would bring with it a demand to confront social stupidity and injustice.

The plays of Shakespeare, which provided an alternative for the English-speaking world to nineteenth-century dramatic rubbish, were burdened with elaborate production details that smothered their perceptions and shut them "up into a museum showcase" (*AC*, 107). Not until the twentieth century did productions "experiment" with something like the original bare stage of Shakespeare's time. Wilder was certain that "when the play is staged as Shakespeare intended it, the bareness of the stage releases the events from the particular and the experience of Juliet partakes of that of all girls in love, in every time, place, and language" (*AC*, 124).

In addition to Shakespeare's creative mastery of the bare stage, Wilder could look to the unadorned play space of the classical Greek theater; to the imaginative genius of one of his own favorite playwrights, Lope de Vega, Shakespeare's contemporary in the Spanish theater; and to the Oriental theater, especially the Chinese, which he knew. He also found encouragement in the theater closer to his own time: in *Six Characters in Search of an Author* the scene is a rehearsal on a bare stage, and the plays of André Obey were performed on a bare stage in the productions of La Compagnie des Quinze under Jacques Copeau.

Perhaps more important to Wilder was the comic play *Ubu the King* by Alfred Jarry, who figured so largely in the avant-garde at the turn of the century. *Ubu the King* achieved its fame through its scandalous first word, *merde* [shit], which obscured the genuine theatrical seriousness of the play. Jarry himself said of it, "The blow against the Great Torturer, Ibsen [read *realism*], passed almost unrecognized."

Jarry, in a letter to the revolutionary actor-director Lugnée-Poë, and later in an essay, described the kind of staging he had in mind for his play. With little change, much of Jarry's scheme could describe the set of *Our Town* as well: ". . . a single set, or better, a plain backdrop (background), omitting the raising and lowering of the curtain . . . a placard signifying the place of the scene. (Note that I am certain of the suggestive superiority of a written placard to scenery.) . . . Costume with as little local color or historical accuracy as possible, . . . modern, preferably. . . ."[19] Jarry justified his insistence on this unusual stage decor: "It is right that each member of the audience sees the scene in the stage-set which agrees with his version of the scene."

He wrote with contempt for all effort at trompe l'oeil, a painted illusion of reality that fools the eye of the beholder, saying that it succeeds only with those who cannot see and offends those who can. Zeuxis, the classical Greek painter, wrote Jarry, created grapes so realistically that it is said birds pecked at them. His skill at illusion was so great that it fooled stupid beasts, and Titian, the Renaissance painter, scarcely much better, tricked an innkeeper.

> The stage set made by those who do not know how to paint comes closer to being abstract in giving the essence of it. . . . [The true set] is obtained simply, by a symbolically exact means, through a back drop not painted, or the opposite of a stage set, everyone seeing through to the *place* he wishes, or better, if the author knows what he wants, the real setting is exosmosed itself on the stage.

Jarry uses somewhat humorously but exactly the term from chemistry, "exosmosis," to describe the process by which the meaningful place will emerge on the stage for the audience through the author's intention and language.

The existence of place in the imagination of the playwright and then through performance in the imagination of the audience became Wilder's aim, too. Like Jarry, he felt that the appearance of the actual objects from the real world diminished any possibility of inner life by "encumbering the stage uselessly." Sometimes the activity of the place demands some particular prop. Wilder took his cue from Jarry here also: "Under these conditions of a bare stage, any part of the set for which there is a special need, a window to be opened, a door to be burst through, is an accessory and can perhaps be carried like a table or a torch." The tables, chairs, trellises and ladders in act 1, and the soda fountain in act 2 are brought on in full view of the audience. By act 3, when Emily returns to her childhood home, even the trellises and chairs and table can be dispensed with. By this time the audience does not need even so little.

Wilder knew the power of the bare stage in the Greek and Renaissance theaters of the past, but it was Jarry's theorizing in a very modern way about the role of the imagination in freeing the stage from the deadening shackles of realistic clutter that showed Wilder the possibilities for a bare stage in his modern theater. Jarry's *Ubu the King* is sardonic and in tone and intention very different from *Our Town*. Yet this strange play touched something vital in Wilder's creative imagination. It continued to fascinate him; when he started thinking about *The Skin of Our Teeth*, his characters were cartoons like those of *Ubu the King,* though ultimately he changed this concept, and in some versions of his last incomplete play *The Emporium,* the characters are also reminiscent of Jarry's.

Wilder's purpose in using the bare stage was, in part, to set his audience free from the meaningless particularity of the box-set. He wrote, "The spectator through lending his imagination to the action restages it inside his own head" (*AC,* 101). But what does the spectator restage? Wilder wrote that "*Our Town* is not offered as a picture of life in a New Hampshire village" (*AC,* 109). So much, then, for the idea that the play is a nostalgic re-creation of a turn-of-the-century small town idyll. Yet Wilder also wrote, "I wished to record a village's life on the stage, with realism and with generality" (*AC,* 101). This apparent contradiction can best be resolved if the words "on the stage" and also the combination of "realism *and* generality" are examined.

The Stage Manager begins *Our Town* by stating that it is a *play* that the audience will see, not reality, and he stresses this idea when he gives the names of the author, producer, director, and actors. And he spells out what the audience will see in the first act: a day in our town. Wilder deliberately calls attention to the information that in most plays is intended to be invisible. We know we are watching a play, but we conspire with the theater to pretend that what we are seeing is the real thing.

In contrast to insisting on the play as play, the Stage Manager speaks of the town as real, providing its name, specific geographical facts, the date, the time of day and description of the physical arrangement of the town, along with the religious and ethnic organization. There are the various churches, and "Polish town's across the tracks, and some Canuck families" (6). The grocery and drug stores are as much a place of meeting and human exchange as of commerce. Then he focuses on the Gibbs and Webb houses and gardens, concluding with "Right here . . . 's a big butternut tree" (7). Although the Stage Manager is very specific about what he is describing, none of the things—except the two trellises, which are pushed out on stage and are suggestive rather than literal—is actually represented on the stage. Insofar as the audience sees any of these things, they must see them in their own imaginations.

It is a "nice" town, but "Nobody very remarkable ever came out of it, s'far as we know" (7). There is no reason to find Grover's Corners interesting because of out-of-the-ordinary events or as a result of some associations between an historical personage and the place. The Stage Manager tells the audience immediately following his disclaimer for the town's being the source of somebody remarkable that the cemetery has the "same names as are around here now" (7). The town is a place of continuity and repetition, not exceptions, but Wilder is also paradoxically denying a sense of the past. There are names, but the names do not convey any sense of personal, individual weight. Writing about Gertrude Stein, Wilder reports that she was struck with the "funny feeling" that dead Americans were not there in the monuments erected to them. Americans do not become "that European thing called 'dead'—so fraught with immemorial connotations" (AC, 210). "Americans do not die, they go away; but . . . they do not go away to their monuments" (AC, 212). So when the Stage Manager offers a snippet of past time: "Bryan once made a speech from these very steps here" (6), the steps do not bring Bryan alive to the audience. They are not a memorial to Bryan dead. Bryan (whatever he may mean to the audience or whatever associations he may have for them) just makes the steps, which are not visible on the stage, more actual, but only as steps that might serve any number of people for speech making, lounging, standing, and so on.

The Stage Manager discusses future time, too. "First automobile's going to come along in about five years" (6). What is peculiar about this future is that it is already past for the audience, providing a kind of double-take. The Stage Manager knows what the audience knows, but what the characters do not. There is no nostalgia for a time before the automobile changed the way we move about; it is a fact. More poignant "facts about everybody" (8) are the deaths in the future of Mrs. Gibbs and Doc Gibbs, who at the moment is very present, "comin' down Main Street now" (8), and of Joe Crowell, who "was awful bright" (10), but who is now delivering newspapers. "The War broke out and he died in France" (10). World War I is, of course, past for the audience. What they glimpse right before their eyes is the youthful promise that will be cut off. "All that education for nothing" (10). Joe Crowell is one of the incomprehensibly melancholy aspects of life in Grover's Corners, though perhaps his death can be seen as a sacrifice to the positive values of the town.

These deaths are presented in the context of other events of the cycle of life. Doc Gibbs has just assisted in the birth of twins. Mrs. Gibbs contracted pneumonia while on a visit West to her married daughter. And Joe Crowell responds to the Stage Manager's humorous question: "Anything serious goin' on in the world since Wednesday?" with the news that "My schoolteacher, Miss Foster, 's getting married" (9). This event in *Our Town is* serious, and it marks the changes of time as surely as death. Joe Crowell, like all young people, is conservative and resists the future: "I think if a person starts out to be a teacher, she ought to stay one" (9).

But Joe Crowell and the other people understand the changes in their individual lives that paradoxically ensure the continuity of life itself. Howie Newsome's horse Bessie cannot understand and adjust. "Bessie's all mixed up about the route ever since the Lockhart's stopped takin' their quart of milk every day. She wants to leave 'em a quart just the same" (11–12).

These apparently trivial events make up the human life cycle of birth, marriage, and death. Joe Crowell's future is sad, not because his education was wasted, but because his participation in life was stopped too soon. Though he shared in life, in itself his individual life is incomplete. Wilder has dramatized the cycle of life by showing us ordinary people participating in it in the ordinary way that is, generally speaking, available to us all.

The individual human cycles are rather small, though of course they are endlessly repeated. One of the ways they can be understood is in the context of bigger developments. The Stage Manager interrupts Mrs. Gibbs and Mrs. Webb to "skip a few hours" (21), and to provide some scientific information about the town. He introduces Professor Willard, reminding him that he must be brief because "unfortunately our time is limited" (21). This remark serves as a comment on the two and one half hours the play takes, but also is a warning true about life itself. Willard, like any academician or anyone else with a captive audience, fails to judge the limits of his listeners' willingness to take in the information of his special interest, and he has to be stopped, providing a bit of gentle comedy. Wilder stresses the idea of time through the Stage Manager, while the Professor provides geological information, again in terms of time—hundreds of millions of years—as well as place. The historical view is the arrival of human inhabitants through waves of immigration beginning with the "Early Amerindian" (22). Including the twins, who have been born that very morning, the population is 2,642, and the mortality and birth rates are constant. Mr. Webb provides a political and social report, including religious denominations of the townsfolk, and he concludes, like the Stage Manager, that the town is "very ordinary" (24). He answers questions from actors planted in the audience about drinking, social and economic injustice, and culture. His answers suggest, not that these conditions do not exist, but that they somehow are irrelevant to any definition of the town, possibly because they are private concerns.

Wilder has very carefully selected the kind of information in this section of act 1 to create a sense of the American that conforms to his ideas, ideas that owe a great deal to Gertrude Stein. The interest in numbers and percentages is, according to Wilder in his essay "Toward an American Language," a peculiarly American dimension. The American enjoys counting, which derives from his disconnection from place.

The American landscape encourages disconnection. Counting "began with his thinking in distances" (*AC*, 17). Americans live "under a sense of boundlessness" (*AC*, 18). Stein explained that "in America there is no sky—there is just air; there is just 'up'; the majority of Americans, in addition, either know the straight line of the sea or the lake, or they know a land so devoid of natural features that 'when they make the boundary of a State they have to make it with a straight line'" (*AC*, 211–12). The "geological facts" of Professor Willard are an attempt to account for all the space in terms of time.

The disconnection from place contains an awareness of vast numbers of people, too. The American "can count to higher numbers—and realize the multiplicity indicated by the number—than any European" (*AC*, 17). "Billions have lived and died, billions will live and die; and this every American knows." But in "American thinking, a crowd of ten thousand is not a homogeneous mass of that number, but is one and one and one . . . up to ten thousand." Mrs. Goruslawski's twins, which add two to the town's population number, are specific individuals. "Each is one" (*AC*, 18).

The "contemplation of the situation of the one in the innumerable . . . sternly forbids . . . any relief from what lies about" (*AC*, 18). Other people and familiar places do not bring any comfortable confirmation of identity. Americans "are exposed to all place and all time" (*AC*, 14). They "hang suspended upon the promises of the imagination. . . . Each one is a bundle of projects" (*AC*, 17–18). Wally Webb has a stamp collection. Mrs. Webb is "putting up" beans. The dream of Mrs. Gibbs's life is to see Paris, France, with Dr. Gibbs. Dr. Gibbs is a Civil War buff, and Mr. Webb follows an interest in Napoleon, though he is tempted "to give up Napoleon and move over to the Civil

War" (20). The townspeople sing together in the church choir. To have a plan brings the consolation to the American that he is irreplaceable.

"There is only one way in which an American can feel himself to be in a relation to other Americans—when he is united with them in a project, caught up in an idea and propelled with them toward the future" (*AC,* 16–17). The townspeople are putting things in the cornerstone of the new bank "for people to dig up . . . a thousand years from now" (32), an activity that combines the ideas of a common project, numbers, and the future. Along with the usual things—newspapers, Shakespeare, the Constitution, and the Bible—the Stage Manager is going to put in a copy of *Our Town,* combining neatly the play as illusion and also its reality. "So . . . the people a thousand years from now'll know a few simple facts about us . . . this is the way we were in the provinces north of New York at the beginning of the twentieth century" (32). The Stage Manager complains that all we know about Babylon, in spite of its two million inhabitants (numbers, again) is "the names of the kings and some copies of wheat contracts. . . . Yet every night all those families sat down to supper, and the father came home from his work, and the smoke went up the chimney,—same as here" (32). When *Our Town* is recovered from the cornerstone a thousand years from now, those people in the future will learn what is important: "This is the way we were: in our growing up and in our marrying and in our living and in our dying" (32). All those verbs are the key activities of the being of Wilder's Americans, and they are participles because, in spite of being past a thousand years from now, the activities they describe happen in a continuous present. And they are, of course, the subject of the play. Wilder's job is to balance the individual experience with multiplicity.

When Mr. Webb is called by the Stage Manager to give his "political and social report" of the lives in *Our Town,* Mrs. Webb appears to explain, "He'll be here in a minute. . . . He just cut his hand while he was eatin' an apple" (23). The actor playing Webb, after a call to hurry from Mrs. Webb and a small effort by the Stage Manager to "fill in" during the delay, finally "enters from his house, pulling on his coat. His finger is bound in a handkerchief" (23). This small event adds nothing to the story or to the characterization of Webb, but it does have significance. There may be a sly reference to Adam and Eve and the apple, one that is a thread throughout Wilder's work. But there is more. Wilder describes a "spiritual exercise" of Gertrude Stein's writing practice: she introduces some phrases from the life around her.

Wilder calls this aspect of her work "the irruption of the daily life" (*AC,* 205). "This resembles," he says, "a practice that her friends the Post-Impressionist painters [such as Picasso] occasionally resorted to. They pasted a subway ticket to the surface of their painting" (*AC,* 205). Though not precisely like Gertrude Stein's method of including overheard conversation in her work or Picasso's use of the pasted ticket, the effect of Webb's cutting his hand is the same. Wilder has invented a reality that appears to be an interruption of the flow of the reality of the play. Of course both the reality of Webb's accident and the "created" reality of Webb's role at this moment in order to tell the audience some facts about the town are wholly Wilder's artifice. Though neither is "real," there is the sense of a juxtaposition of two kinds of reality. The aim is to produce a shock and to lend vitality to the illusion of Webb at this moment. Wilder employs this artiface elsewhere, too, as when the Stage Manager interrupts Professor Willard for going on at too great length with pedantic facts about "Professor Gruber's notes on the meteorological situation" (21); when he whispers to Willard about the birth of the twins, about which he has just learned, and the consequent rise in the population by two; when the actors planted as members of the audience ask questions; and when the Stage Manager shifts chairs to make the drug store soda fountain. At all these times the illusion of the realism of the play is broken by another reality, and paradoxically it is strengthened in its meaning. The audience is not allowed for very long to get caught up in the singular events of the characters before being forced to confront the truth that they are watching a performance in a theater, and its very importance is that it is a performance.

"In my plays . . . ," wrote Wilder in his *Journals,* "there is this constant interruption. The more I seek to exhibit an idea about life, the more I must make sure that the tumult of sheer existences be introduced, pertinent and impertinent . . . , and the more I start out to give an instance of some character's individual action, the more I lift it from the specific-unique into the realm of the typical and the idea-expressive" (*J,* 329).

After Webb answers the questions from the audience, the Stage Manager returns the scene to the town, now in the afternoon, with the children coming home from school. Emily and George are at the age when they are beginning to be aware of their future as adults. Emily is perhaps more anxiously conscious than George is. George is still a boy, "throwing a ball up to dizzying heights" (27) and bumping into people on the street. He, without envy, admires Emily's success at school; he has problems with algebra and looks forward to being free of school to work on his Uncle Luke's farm, which he can "just gradually have" (29). George is not so much thoughtless as he is entirely comfortable in the world he has been given. He does not anticipate any difficulties to which he will not be equal.

Emily seems more aware of choices, though she is as comfortable with being "just naturally bright" (28) as George is with ball playing that gradually will give way to farming. Emily has made a "fine speech in class" (27), and she is "going to make speeches all [her] life" (30). Though her speech making and George's ball playing reveal something about them, these activities only indirectly prepare them for their adult lives. Emily is beginning to feel the peril of approaching womanhood, a justified anxiety, because as act 3 makes clear, the peril is real. But for now the tone is light, even comic. Her manner of walking as she returns from school gives "some signs that she is imagining herself to be a lady of startling elegance" (26), foolishness that her father not unkindly deflates. The promptings that lead her to this comic imagining, that make her aware that school is some sort of development, "something you have to go through" and that "passes the time" (28), are certainly part of the passing of time that is further developed by the news that George will eventually have a farm and by her mother's comment that George is growing up. Emily helps her mother string beans (an activity that was comically misunderstood in a French production where the two actresses busily threaded *haricots verts* with a needle, as though they were beads). When Emily asks her mother if she's "pretty enough . . . to get people interested" (31) in her, Wilder is dramatizing an appealing mixture of childish vanity and human sexual necessity. The preparation of the beans, unlike the speech making, is more directly connected with Emily's future. Her mother's reply, "You're pretty enough for all normal purposes" (31), is a general truth, but a frustrating answer to the individual Emily. She is feeling what every girl feels, but every girl's feeling is unique to herself, as though she were the first one. Emily asks her mother if *she* had been pretty as a girl. Here is the idea of repeated generations. Mrs. Webb's answer about herself, "Yes, I was, if I do say it. I was the prettiest girl in town next to Mamie Cartwright" (31), is the kind of description every girl wants for herself. Mrs. Webb's honesty, somewhat humorously, makes her admit Mamie Cartwright's superiority in prettiness but also helps us believe that Mrs. Webb is speaking the truth apart from mere vulgar vanity. However, the real humor and truth come from the very different sorts of answers she gives to the two questions. Emily is "pretty enough." "All *my* children have got good features." "You have a nice young pretty face" (30). But, "*I* was the prettiest girl in town" (my italics). Mrs. Webb thinks of Emily as representative, but of herself as a unique individual. She is at the same time acting out of general motherly care to prevent her child from the dangers of vanity, much as Webb is doing when he gently teases Emily about her grand lady manner. Any production that has the choice should select an actress to play Emily who can create the illusion of ravishing, though innocent, youthful loveliness. Mrs. Webb's words to Emily should seem neither mean nor stupid. The two different kinds of answer are another dramatic version of the two aspects of human experience that Wilder presents. George and Emily are specific characters in the play, but they dramatize the universal situation of the beginning of human adulthood. They are everybody, too, as indeed is Mrs. Webb.

The concluding scenes to act 1 demonstrate how well Wilder understood the possibilities for poetry of the theater on a bare stage. Throughout act 1 Wilder indicated sounds to help create the illusion: a train whistle, clinking milk bottles, a factory whistle, chickens cackling. These sounds all mark some shift in focus in the play. The train whistle suggests a world away from the town and also marks time, widening the perspective to include death. The milk bottles are part of both the stability and the change found in the routine of morning delivery. The chickens, somewhat comically, fill a pause that shifts attention from the ordinary in Mrs. Gibbs and Mrs. Webb's morning chatter to the extraordinary possibility of selling a highboy to a Boston antiques dealer and using the money to travel abroad, suggesting again that world that exists around and apart from the town. The train whistle is almost a poetic cliché in drama, but the other sounds are not so usual.

The last section of act 1 begins with the singing of the hymn "Blessed Be the Tie That Binds." Almost everybody recognizes the power in the plainness and simplicity of the best of Protestant hymns. They stir feelings directly and artlessly. Hymn singing seems peculiarly and identifiably American, though often the hymns sung are not American in origin. The stage is in darkness, except for spots that pick out the characters when they are part of the scene. The combination of nighttime and music and sounds (the crickets) is just about fool-proof. It is difficult to resist the subliminal mood that envelopes the characters' speeches. Shakespeare, the master of just about every theater technique, skillfully used just such combinations, sometimes with real sounds and music, as in the scene in *Antony and Cleopatra* where Hercules leaves Antony, and sometimes using words to create the sounds as well as the night, as in the opening of act 5 of *The Merchant of Venice*, where Jessica and Lorenzo try to "out-night" each other with word painting. Chekhov, closer to Wilder in time, created magical theatrical effects with sounds and lighting. In Chekhov's *The Sea Gull*, of which Wilder wrote an acting version later in his career, there is apart from the realism a combination of moonlight and music that is identical, though for a different end, with the mood in *Our Town*. Wilder wrote in his *Journals* that in *Our Town* the "suggestibility of the imagined scene . . . was accompanied by a studied resort to changes of lighting." He was not entirely happy about his dependence upon the lights. "I intend in this play [*The Emporium*] to deny myself the aid of shifting lights. The challenge to the audience's imagination will be still bolder . . ." (*J*, 43). Though the lighting is exceptionally effective in production, it really is not necessary. The exclamations about the moonlight that punctuate the dialogue successfully evoke an imagined scene.

The moonlight and music unite the characters with a common experience. They also lift the attention of the characters and the audience to a wider context than the specific concerns of algebra and chores about the house. The Stage Manager says that "time's gone by. It's evening" to set the time of day and also to call attention to time's passing. "The day's running down like a tired clock" (33). George and Emily remain on the ladders that have been pushed out on the stage almost throughout. They begin the evening, Emily helping George with his algebra. She is moved by the *terrible* moonlight, though George seems hardly aware of it. The moonlight affects Emily so powerfully partly because her homework is no trouble and partly because she is susceptible to the romance of the night, including the sound of the distant train. George is less aware of these wider perspectives because his attention is focused on his difficulty with schoolwork. He, however, weeps when his father calls his attention to how hard his mother works for him, even doing the chores that should be his. This marks George's second failure to act on what is around him. However, George is not unaware and unfeeling; he seems to be fixed on inner disturbances, caused by his growing awareness of Emily. He watches her, nights, from his window. Almost as though he does not know why she attracts him, he expresses his admiration practically, by asking for her aid. His weeping is also an expression, moving, but somewhat comic as well, of his awareness that he is not living up to life's potential, though George does not understand it in these terms. Only Emily in act 3 can give expression to such unspecific sorrow.

The audience has been "softened" by the music and the terrible moonlight to accept the emotion prompted by what is apparently so small. Dr. Gibbs, instead of scolding George, allows George's perception to arise within him. Dr. Gibbs then changes the subject to a rise in allowance and finally expresses his own discomfort at having made George weep by complaining against the choir, which has been singing softly throughout his exchange with George. He is particularly irritated by his wife's singing in spite of having no "more voice than an old crow" (37). This small comedy, like that when Stimson suggests that since music should be pleasure, the choir should leave loudness to the Methodists, works against sentimentality, but even the references to the choir, apart from the singing, maintain the function of the choir as a unifying device. Wilder has even carefully chosen his hymns for their general sentiments, apart from their Christian message. "Blessed Be the Tie That Binds" celebrates the common experience. "Art Thou Weary; Art Thou Languid?" asks the question that is implied in Gibbs's talk with George.

Meanwhile we see the choir from varying perspectives. Stimson, when he asks the choir to sing at a wedding—just as they did last month—lightly develops the themes of marriage and repetition that began with Joe Crowell and will get fuller expression in act 2. The women, returning from choir practice, convey their pleasure simply in singing together. They also react to the moonlight. Mrs. Gibbs deflates its romantic aspects by concluding it means "Potato weather, for sure" (38). But she responds to its beauty when she also calls to her husband to "Come out and smell the heliotrope in the moonlight" (39). Mrs. Soames, who is more ordinary, says the moonlight is "as bright as day," and she can even "see Mr. Soames scowling at the window" (39).

Rebecca shares George's window, because there is no moon at her own. She "thinks" that the moon is closing on the earth and there will be a "big 'splosion." This universal catastrophe shifts to the thought that the moon is shining on "half the whole world" (41–42). Either way, the human group is for the moment united by the moon.

Rebecca's fear that the moon will collide with the earth in a calamitous explosion has no basis in reality. George, though perhaps his faith in experts is naive, though very American, points out that if it were true, "the guys that sit up all night with telescopes would . . . tell about it, and it'd be in all the newspapers" (42). However, Wilder's world is not an idyll free from difficulty. Throughout this section run Simon Stimson's unhappiness and alcoholism as a variation in a minor key. Stimson also serves to distinguish characters from each other through their reactions to him. Mrs. Soames is eager to gossip and disapproves of Stimson. Refusing to enjoy another's unhappiness, Mrs. Gibbs puts the blame for his drinking on his "troubles"; and Mrs. Webb falsely insists that "It's getting better" (38). But when Mrs. Gibbs is alone with her husband, she reveals that she thinks the problem is a serious one. Dr. Gibbs, and later Webb, sympathize with Stimson's sorrow though they conclude that there is "nothing we can do but just leave it alone" (40). Dr. Gibbs claims that he knows "more about Simon Stimson's affairs than anybody in this town" (40), but neither he nor anyone else ever offers any specific facts about Stimson's troubles. Wilder dramatizes profound unhappiness in general, much the way he uses the bare stage, rather than providing some particular cause from which the audience can comfortably separate itself. Nonetheless, Wilder is making some observations about human unhappiness that go further than a mere acknowledgement that it exists, and he is deepening the themes in his play.

Dr. Gibbs, to explain Stimson's situation, says "Some people ain't made for small-town life" (40). He means exactly what he says, that some people are stifled by the narrow environment of the actual small town and are more comfortable with the excitement and stimulation that the modern city provides. But Wilder is using life in Grover's Corners as "the way we were—at the beginning of the twentieth century" (32), and Stimson must have some relation to life in general. He is a musician, and music is important enough that he chooses "some notes of music" (85) as the epitaph on his gravestone. He is a kind of romantic artist, dissatisfied and critical of ordinary living. This is a cliché, of course, and we might be impatient with it if Wilder allowed it any greater individual importance than he does.

Writing in his *Journals* two years after the success of *Our Town*, Wilder distinguished between catastrophes in the external world of nature and those in the subjective world of the mind. The catastrophes in the external world are not a source of tragedy because they are largely regular in occurrence, and "Tragedy enters with the irregular" (*J*, 32). He dismissed exceptional events, like earthquakes, and those that are evitable, like illness, as having less importance. It is the subjective world that results from man's possession of consciousness that interests Wilder more. I shall consider in greater detail the nature of man's attitude toward death in the discussion of act 3, but it should be noted here that Wilder concludes:

> except in certain periods of history, the prevailing judgment of man has repudiated the attitude that the inevitability of death is sufficient grounds to affirm that all life is in itself an ill. The significant pessimism in the world's testimony enters with the two-fold charge that man's nature—expressed in his possession of consciousness— is (1) inharmonious in itself, and (2) incapable of giving or receiving a true satisfaction from its relations with other consciousnesses.
>
> (*J*, 32)

Later in his *Journals,* "overwhelmed by accounts of neurotic woe" (182) from his friends, Wilder mulled over these two inharmonious conditions of man's nature:

> Now let us not be afraid of clichés. . . . [These friends were] Starved of the environment of love: hence forever after exhibiting so greedy and omnivorous an expectation of love that no affection they *receive* is adequate, and (what is worse) their affection for others is not truly love but a demand and a command to be loved. . . . man, such as he is, has no choice but to believe, to insist on believing, that the world is grounded in love—love as affection.
>
> (*J*, 182–83)

Consciousness of the gap between what man desires both from himself and from outside himself and what he thinks he receives, which is the civilized human condition and exists to a greater degree in artists, can lead the "exceptional person" to comment pessimistically about the "exceptional experience"—in other words, Stimson's reaction to his "peck of troubles." But for Wilder, no great works of art assert this pessimism. Using Voltaire and Swift for his evidence for harsh pictures of mankind, he concludes that these writers imply "not man's unalterable disharmony . . . but the failure of man to take advantage of his possibilities of good" (*J*, 33). Stimson is—and Wilder has no explanation—the neurotic who is disposed to pessimism and who denies that his ills are correctable. When Dr. Gibbs concludes, "I don't know how that'll end; but there's nothing we can do but just leave it alone" (40), he is not being hard-hearted or indifferent or demonstrating a lack of imagination; he is expressing Wilder's views about the "unloving demanders-of-love" (*J*, 186). The source of their unhappiness is a rejection of affection. Their despair is an expression of "the *insoluble* problem of the mind at war with the body; and the *incorrectable* presence of the self-destructive element in the social group" (*J*, 33; my italics). Dr. Gibbs is realistic, but not without sympathy.

Stimson has rejected life and its possibilities, and his suicide serves as his final act of rejection. Wilder in his use of Stimson distinguishes himself from Stimson's kind of artist. Stimson is "employed to light up the noble aspects of human nature; man's *good* is affirmed by man's ever present but partial ill" (*J*, 33). Stimson's failure in living throws in relief the struggle, however inadequate, of the other characters to seize time. His drunken silence when Webb offers to walk with him, like his music and his unhappiness with small-town life, has an accurate particular actuality, but Wilder is also symbolically dramatizing the inability to accept or even acknowledge human affection.

The act ends with Emily still gazing at the moon, her father whistling "Blessed Be the Tie That Binds," and Rebecca telling George about Jane Crofut's letter: "on the envelope the address was like this: It said: Jane Crofut; The Crofut Farm; Grover's Corners; Sutton County; New Hampshire; United States of America . . . it's not finished: the United States of America; Continent of North America; Western Hemisphere; the Earth; the Solar System; the Universe; the Mind of God—that's what it said on the envelope" (45). The idea of the address on Jane Crofut's letter was certainly suggested by the passage in James Joyce's *A Portrait of the Artist as a Young Man*, where Stephen "turned to the flyleaf of the geography and read what he had written there: himself, his name and where he was.

> Stephen Dedalus
> Class of Elements
> Clongowes Wood College
> Sallins
> County Kildare
> Ireland

Europe
The World
The Universe."

In Joyce the list of ever larger places seems increasingly claustrophobic, as though Stephen's imagination repeatedly confronts new restrictions, from which there is no escape to freedom. "What was after the universe?" Stephen asks, and he answers, "Nothing." It made "him very tired to think that way."[20]

Jane Crofut's address, in contrast, is exhilarating to George and Rebecca. It enumerates ever expanding possibilities for the individual Jane Crofut, and indeed, for every member of the audience. "And the postman brought it just the same" (45). Jane is not trapped, but neither is she lost, not here on the Crofut Farm and not in the Mind of God. The farm possesses a specific actuality. The Mind of God is the widest possible category of imagination and thought, combining abstraction and enormous perspective.

"What do you know!" (45) exclaims George, and his expression is comically inadequate, lyrically and intellectually. But it touchingly conveys his genuine sense of amazed wonder. And when the Stage Manager announces that this is the end of the first act, he is speaking the literal truth and bringing the audience back to the idea of the play itself. He is also calling attention to the general truth that has been presented in act 1. All the details and activities of living daily life, as well as the generalized events, are found in the mysterious imaginative force of the Universe, to which they lend and from which they derive meaning.

5

Love and Marriage

At the beginning of act 1, when the Stage Manager identifies and describes the places in *Our Town* and tells of events in the past and the future, he sets the imaginations of the audience wandering, so that they help bring Grover's Corners to life. It is every day in every life everywhere. The second act is "called Love and Marriage" (47), and it also takes place in a day in the life of Grover's Corners, so much of the beginning is similar to but slightly different from the first act. The perspective is still that of "a thousand years from now" (32), of the people who will dig up the cornerstone of the Cartwright Bank.

When the second act begins, time has passed—three years, more than a thousand sun-rises—and changes have occurred. The mountains are "cracked . . . a little bit more" (46); there are new children; and some people have noticed they are a bit older. These changes are natural, and "Nature's been pushing and contriving in other ways, too: a number of young people fell in love and got married" (46). Wilder directly links the wearing away of the mountains and the sunrises with marriage as events of Nature. They are changes, they do make differences, and they are repeated events. "Almost everybody in this world gets married" (46).

Wilder wrote in his introduction to Gertrude Stein's *Narration* that repeating is characteristic of all life. He quoted from Stein's text: "If a thing is really existing there can be no repetition. . . . Then we have insistence insistence that in its emphasis can never be repeating, because insistence is always alive and if it is alive it is never saying anything in the same way because emphasis can never be the same not even when it is most the same that is when it has been taught" (*AC*, 183–84). Repeating is not simply the same thing again. It is "insistence," or life, because nothing ever really happens exactly the same way again. The focus is on its happening. Again Wilder quoted from Gertrude Stein: "The only time that repeating is really repeating, that is when it is dead, is when something is being taught" (*AC*, 191). There is a kind of dead repeating, but that happens only when it comes close to being the same, when it is being taught, or has been learned, but does not emerge from experience. Otherwise repeating is creative, and it can suggest some sort of progression.

The day's beginning is repeated, but Wilder calls attention to changes. The train whistle is heard. "Only this time it's been raining. It's been pouring and thundering" (47). "River's been risin' all night" (49). In the light of what have become clichés of anthropology and myth in literature, all this water seems appropriate to the wedding as a fertility ritual. And the flood, if not seriously a reference to the life-giving flooding of the Nile, or the new beginning promised by Noah's flood, is at least fitting to the youthful passion of Emily and George.

This morning "there's Si Crowell delivering the papers like his brother before him" (48). Si objects to the changes brought by George's marriage just as his brother objected to his teacher's marriage: "we're losing about the best baseball pitcher Grover's Corners ever had—George Gibbs" (48). But Constable Warren puts even this change in the perspective of repeating. "Back in '84 we had a player, Si—even George Gibbs couldn't touch him. . . . Went down to Maine and become a Parson" (49).

Though Howie Newsome is still delivering the milk, the Webbs and the Gibbses need more now because of the expected wedding guests. The stirrings in the two households are much the same as usual, though Wilder will present a day differing in detail from that in the first act. "Mrs. Gibbs and Mrs. Webb come down to make breakfast, just as though it were an ordinary day" (47). And though the Stage Manager says that he does not have to point out the dependable regularity of wife/mothers to provide for their families, he in fact does so. Their living and their efforts to maintain the life of their families are one and the same. Neither they nor women like them have had a nervous breakdown, which is a testimony to their heroic strength and to what is basically correct in their living. Wilder knows, just as every-body else knows, that there is a great variety of ways for individual women (and men) to live their lives; not all must have children and devote themselves to caring for them. He is dramatizing cooking, laundering, ordering a home as essential human functions, and if some women are novelists or presidents, who cannot or choose not to per-form these activities, someone else *must* perform them. Life, including writing novels and being presidents, depends on them. It is sentimental to regard any other activities as having the same weight and impor-tance. The Stage Manager concludes with the idea that having and loving life are the same things. "It's what they call a vicious cycle" (47). The cliché, because it is a cliché, softens the harshness of *vicious* in laughter, but Wilder is also stating that making a virtue of necessity does not change the brutality of the necessity. We humans, Stein and Wilder agree, are victims of biology.

Stein, in her extraordinary novel, *The Making of Americans*, ob-served, "Repeating is the whole of living and by repeating comes un-derstanding, and understanding is to some the most important part of living. Repeating is the whole of living, and it makes living a thing always more familiar to each one. . . ."[21] Repeating is essential to liv-ing; it is in nature; it is a sign of life. What results from repeating for some, according to this passage, is understanding. The repeating is the "struggle of the human mind in its work, which is to know" (*AC*, 221). Repeating is the activity of *Our Town*'s characters; it is their effort to understand. Natural repetition is Nature's struggle to bring into being some knowledge of itself.

The Stage Manager says about marriage, "Once in a thousand times it's interesting." Wilder is not demeaning marriage or all the in-dividuals who are married. He is echoing Stein's notion of *interesting*. It is the "vitality enough of knowing enough of what you mean," when "you know what you mean and so . . . you mean what you know, what you know you mean" (*AC*, 202). When "all the small occasions in the daily life" are known (and understood) as though they had never happened to anyone else ever before. What is *interesting* is the struggle of the Human Mind to free itself from the accustomed and to confront what Gertrude Stein called *ugliness* or the newness of a thing. To do it as though for the first time. It is only one in a thousand times that individuals in a marriage are aware through repeating of what is ex-citing in their marriage and who can thereby maintain something that is lively and perhaps even new. George and Emily begin as though for the first time. Their fears reveal their new experience. We never really know whether their marriage is interesting.

The abstract idea of marriage that is presented in act 2 is prompted in part by G. B. Shaw's ideas about marriage in, for example, *Man and Superman*. Wilder used as well as responded to Shaw's notion of the Life Force, "the force that ever strives to attain greater power of contemplating itself."[22] The Life Force is very similar to Stein's Human Mind.

In the summer of 1928 Wilder and Gene Tunney, the champion boxer, hiked through France and into Italy. Despite the unlikely combination, Tunney's eager interest in literature and Wilder's physical enthusiasm created a bond between the two men, and they hit it off. Before going on to France, they met in England, where they visited Shaw. Shaw had boxed in his youth and maintained an interest in boxing throughout his life, so his willingness to meet Tunney is not strange. But for Wilder, the encounter was not a success. Shaw apparently did not like Wilder and condescendingly snubbed him. Wilder later wrote that Shaw had harangued them, showing none of his reputed gaiety and fun. Wilder attributed Shaw's behavior to his essential shyness and his dependence on the reaction of others. He concluded that Shaw insulted others in order to provoke them. Wilder many years later wrote an essay on Shaw, which was not published until after his death, and since Wilder did not write very much about authors who were not important to him—except for some brief speeches that were intended for a specific occasion—it is certain that despite Shaw's social snub, he was important to Wilder intellectually. It would be a mistake to identify Shaw exclusively with the "European fella" (71) mentioned by the Stage Manager, but Shaw is certainly one of the inclusive identifications. In my own conversations with Wilder Shaw is the only playwright I can remember apart from Shakespeare that he brought up himself.

It is necessary to keep in mind how different Wilder is from Shaw in spite of shared intellectual interests in the idea of marriage and man's struggle to improve humanity. First Wilder lacks all of Shaw's polemical-reformer traits. Wilder believed firmly that "misery and inhumanity never sleep, nor are they so easily abolished; they merely displace themselves" (*AC*, 91). Because of an "incomplete conception of the human need" (*AC*, 91), according to Wilder, "Shaw attacked the institution of marriage," whose strengths Wilder praised throughout his career, though he was not blind to its unhappy aspects. And, of course, he never married himself. Wilder, taking his cue from Shaw's own claim to be in dramatic dialogue with Shakespeare, felt that though Shaw was successful in his presentation of erratic young women, because he had no "instinctive sympathetic understanding of the nature of woman" (*AC*, 91), he, unlike Shakespeare, except in some few scenes like the first act of *Heartbreak House,* was unable to "present a young woman as both virtuous and interesting" (*AC*, 93).

Emily is surely Wilder's attempt to present such a young woman. It does not matter whether Wilder's thoughts on Shaw are "correct" or not; they help us to understand Wilder's aims. His description of the qualities of Shakespeare's young women define Wilder's own ideal: "they are unafraid, resourceful, observant, and thoughtful, and they are singularly exempt from the notion that they ceased to have any significance save in relation to some man. All of them are finally married, but we have the sense that they would have remained no less the objects of our admiration had we known them many years later as spinsters" (*AC*, 93).

Emily resembles more Wilder's description of Shakespeare's heroine than she does the "erratic young woman" of Shaw's plays, but she, and George, too, are in the same human predicament as Ann Whitefield and Jack Tanner in *Man and Superman*.

Shaw's lovers have some sense of reenacting a human pattern. Tanner in his unconventional proposal to Ann in act 4 says, "(Struck by the echo from the past) When did all this happen to me before? Are we two dreaming?"[23] He is remembering the "dream" of act 3 where he is Don Juan and Ann is Dona Ana, from Mozart's *Don Giovanni* among other versions of the Don Juan story, but he is also expressing some sense of his own repeating part within life's pattern. Wilder does not allow George and Emily any such awareness, but he knows what Tanner glimpses. George and Emily are not descendents of such illustrious ancestors as Don Juan and Dona Ana. But they do enact a life pattern that is so often repeated that it shares in the power of myth. Since they are Americans, as I shall show, they must appear to themselves to do it for the first time.

Wilder and Shaw share the view that the pattern produces change, and that change is often improvement. This is partly what Ann means when she tells Octavius: "Oh, that's poetry, Tavy. . . . It gives me that sudden sense of an echo from a former existence which always seems to me such a striking proof that we have immortal souls."[24] This time around Dona Ana will not marry Don Ottavio; she will make a better selection in Don Juan–Tanner. In retelling the story to give Dona Ana a better, more suitable match, Shaw moves the human race ahead. The Stage Manager makes much the same point about the expectations of the past for a better future. "And don't forget all the other witnesses at this wedding,—the ancestors. Millions of them. Most of them set out to love two-by-two, also. Millions of them" (71).

George and Emily cannot escape any more than Tanner and Ann. Mrs. Gibbs says, "people are meant to go through life two by two. "'Tain't natural to be lonesome" (53). And the Stage Manager repeats later, for emphasis: "Like Mrs. Gibbs said a few minutes ago: People were meant to live two-by-two" (71). He offers it as the explanation for the idea that marriage is a sacrament. Don Juan says somewhat more forcefully, "Life seized me and threw me into her [Woman's] arms as a sailor throws a scrap of fish into the mouth of a seabird."[25] With more enthusiasm, Tanner says later when he embraces Ann, "The Life Force enchants me: I have the whole world in my arms when I clasp you."[26] Both playwrights are dramatizing the power of human biological inevitability, but Wilder accepts it and Shaw attempts to expose it to an audience that disguised and disfigured it with sentimental nonsense.

The purpose of biology in Shaw is to create a better human being, not love and beauty. "Life is a force which has made innumerable experiments in organizing itself . . . to build up that raw force into higher and higher individuals."[27] The weddings in Grover's Corners are not ceremonies of love and beauty either, in spite of Mrs. Soames's repeated exclamation about how lovely the wedding of George and Emily is. They are "awfully plain and short" (71). The Stage Manager says before the wedding, "The real hero of this scene isn't on the stage at all, and you know who that is. It's like what one of those European fellas [Shaw, certainly, though not only he] said: every child born into the world is nature's attempt to make a perfect human being. . . . nature's interested in . . . quality" (71).

The repeating that Wilder portrayed in human existence is part of the acting style, too. The miming of activities without props was the most startling innovation in the performance of the play. It seemed as strange as the bare stage, to which it is related in style. The actors mime preparing breakfast, stringing beans, feeding the chickens, mowing the grass, delivering the paper and milk, activities that in life are repeated daily or seasonally. The pantomime was recognized by some in the original audience as something like the style of Chinese theater, where an actor might appear, for example, walking in a bobbing gait in circles with a whip in his hand, and be recognized immediately as being on a journey on horseback. Perhaps they were remembering *The Yellow Jacket* by George C. Hazelton and Benrimo, a popular success that had self-consciously reproduced some of the characteristics of Chinese theater. Though Wilder lived for two extended periods of his childhood in China, where his father was Consul General, first at Hong Kong and then at Shanghai, he apparently never saw a full-length performance of a Chinese play, either as a child or as an adult. But he did see one of the extraordinary and celebrated performances of the great Chinese actor Mei Lan-fang. Undoubtedly the impact of this great actor's skill and style impressed on Wilder the profound power of performing actions without props.

Stark Young, translator, teacher, and critic, described some of the impact of Mei Lan-fang apart from Mei's illusionist skill. He wrote more generally about theatrical convention:

> When purely symbolistic, these conventions represent—without re-producing—ideas, actions, things, exactly as words do, which in themselves are nothing but sound. There is this difference, however, between these symbols and words: a movement or object symbol-izing a beautiful idea, personage, place, tends to be created into something in itself more beautiful and worthy of the association, whereas a word remains the same, plus perhaps our efforts to put beauty into its employment. These conventions in themselves have doubtless, therefore, taken on a greater and greater perfection.[28]

The pantomime in *Our Town* is, as Stark Young suggests Mei Lan-fang's movements were, a symbolistic representation of truth.

In the *New York Times* in 1938 Wilder wrote: "The theatre longs to represent the symbols of things, not the things themselves. All the lies it tells . . . all those lies enhance the one truth that is there—the truth that dictated the story, the myth."[29] Later Wilder recorded in his *Journals:* "every work of the imagination is a construction of sym-bols" (*J*, 218). Though this is not the place for a detailed discussion of that very complicated word *symbol,* it is important to distinguish between Wilder's use of the term "symbol" here and the usual loose definition as some device containing a complex of events, ideas, or feelings, as, for example, the cross as a symbol of Christianity. The ideal actors in a performance of *Our Town* do not identify with the characters; they represent them or show them. The actors are not an illusion of real people, but symbols of the characters, just as the characters and their actions are symbols of some human truth that can be contemplated in a way that chaotic life cannot. Or as Stark Young says about words and Mei's movements: they represent without reproducing.

The pantomime is part of Wilder's larger view of the ideal manner and function of acting and what it contributes to the play. He wrote:

> Should an actor convey to the audience that he is "really" terrified or heartbroken or even amused, the scene in which he was playing would immediately lose all illusion. . . . all the attention would be centered on him, . . . which has nothing to do with the inner action of the play. Acting is not experiencing but describing and indicating a reality.
>
> So all art has the passions and the states-of-being for subject matter; its function, however, is to contemplate them, to show them, and not to be them.
>
> (*J*, 6)

Stark Young continued about Mei Lan-fang,

> What we must say about the realism and abstraction and stylization of Mei Lan-fang's art is that, exactly as is the case in the classic Chinese art, we are astonished at the precision of its realistic notations and renderings, and are dazzled by the place these take in the highly stylized and removed whole that the work of art becomes . . . none of these is impersonation or reality in the usual sense. They are real only in the sense that great sculptures or paintings are real, through their motion in repose, their impression of shock, brief duration and beautiful finality. Every now and then—very rarely—in acting we see this happen: I mean a final quality in some emotion, the presentation of that truth which confirms and enlarges our sense of reality.[30]

The relation understood by Stark Young between "realistic notations and renderings" and the stylized whole is another version of the one and many that obsessed Wilder. In his *Journals*, after observing that Gogol's hero in *Dead Souls* "is very nearly an Everyrussian (and so joins that company of [Joyce's] Bloom, Earwicker, and Kafka's K.—the hero of the novel of the future)," he concludes, "the more a central figure represents a universal, the more the author must construct an ambiance which furnishes indications and intimations of everything, everywhere, everybody and everyhow" (*J*, 192).

Although Wilder recognized the ironic and droll character of Gogol's intent to be different from his own, he also observed that the device Gogol used to lend a philosophical character was the *"excessively specific in non-pertinent situations"* (*J*, 191). The modern writer cannot include every detail of the life of Everyman, so he isolates one particular, startling detail: "Aesthetically, they convey a sense of the innumerability of persons and objects in the world" (*J*, 191). This irrelevant detail "says that out of the billions of things that are present in the world surrounding my selected story-subject, I introduce, *without reason,* this *one.* And with that 'one' the door is for a moment opened to all the others" (*J*, 193).

The pantomime both of Mei Lan-fang and of *Our Town* isolates a specific realistic detail in such a way that its part in a universal truth can be acknowledged and contemplated. The milk delivery is not interesting in itself, and it does not advance the plot. The audience is arrested by it because of its peculiar presentation, and they should come to recognize its abstract importance to the idea of living—if not before, but certainly by act 3, when so many of the familiar townspeople are dead.

In Wilder's kind of theater the actor must present the character. If he actually offers himself and his thoughts and feelings to the audience, he is in effect replacing the play with himself. Many actors have been tempted into expanding their roles by adding business and even dialogue; it looks easy to do. It inevitably damages the play, which has been carefully planned in every detail. The mime is part of the presentation style.

Wilder had firsthand experience on the stage, acting in his own plays, though he never suggested that he thought he had mastered the profession. His humorous advice to young actors who asked for help in performing in his plays was to find a place where they could speak very loud and then do it. But he had also considered more seriously what acting required. In *Some Thoughts on Playwriting* he distinguished three separate faculties that together made up the actor's gift: observation, imagination, and physical coordination. The way in which he described these three faculties applies in a helpful way to the mime in *Our Town*.

> 1. An observant and analyzing eye for all modes of behavior about us, for dress and manner, and for the signs of thought and emotion in oneself and in others.

The actor must have the capacity to see what people do physically, and then to understand what those actions reveal about inner states.

> 2. The strength of imagination and memory whereby the actor may, at the indication in the author's text, explore his store of observations and represent the details of appearance and the intensity of the emotions—joy, fear, surprise, grief, love, and hatred—and through imagination extend them to intenser degrees and to differing characterizations.

He must have the power to remember what he has observed and the imagination to intensify it and to apply it properly to the text.

> 3. A physical coordination whereby the force of these inner realizations may be communicated to voice, face, and body.
>
> (*AC*, 119)

This last is most important: an actor "must physically *express* his knowledge," that is, he must represent the character through the means of his body on stage.

Wilder admired the work of Richard Boleslavsky, who directed his first play. Boleslavsky was an emigré from Russia who trained with the prerevolutionary Moscow Art Theater, and his theories for training actors are based on that tradition. The author-critic Francis Fergusson, who worked with Boleslavsky in the American Laboratory Theatre, is surely right when he says that, although he was active in American theater and movies, Boleslavsky's teaching is his major legacy to us.

In his book *Acting, the First Six Lessons*, Boleslavsky encourages his acting student to reproduce in pantomime without the aid of props the simplest sorts of everyday activities: pouring tea, for example. This method of training was based on a German kindergarten game called

Achtungspiele. Like the characters in *Our Town*, Boleslavsky's students were busily pantomiming everyday activities that they observed in themselves and in others. Boleslavsky wrote that "It helps a student of the theatre to notice everything unusual and out of the ordinary in every-day life. It builds his memory . . . with all visible manifestations of the human spirit. It makes him sensitive to sincerity and to make-believe. It develops his sensory and muscular memory . . . it enriches his inner life by full and extensive consumption of everything in outward life."[31]

Wilder's three faculties of the actor are an echo of Boleslavsky's advantages to be derived from the actor's exercise of observation and re-creation of what he has observed. More important to Wilder's idea of what is represented on the stage is the relationship Boleslavsky noted between "visible manifestations" and "the human spirit"; "sincerity" and "make-believe"; and the "outward life" and the "inner life." He thought of these things functioning in the service of the success of the actor's performance. It is these very things that Wilder wants to show on his stage. What Wilder recognized was that acting was presenting living in such a way that it could be recognized apart from any other goal. Mr. Webb pushes his imaginary lawn mower, not in the service of the plot—which might require that he die of cardiac arrest so that Mrs. Webb can be free to go to New York to marry her lover—but to show Webb *being* a middle-aged husband and father. The pantomime is a theatrical convention that allows the re-creation "within the imagination of each of the spectators" of daily living. "It provokes the collaborative activity of the spectator's imagination; and . . . [i]t raises the action from the specific to the general" (*AC*, 124), which are constantly Wilder's aims.

The pantomime is an appropriate sort of acting for the bare stage. Wilder knew that the theater "lives by conventions: a convention is an agreed-upon falsehood, a permitted lie. . . . The stage is a fundamental pretense and it thrives on the acceptance of that fact and in the multiplication of additional pretenses. When it tries to assert that the personages in the action 'really are,' really inhabit such-and-such rooms, really suffer such-and-such emotions, it loses rather than gains credibility" (*AC*, 122–23). An actual lawn mower for Mr. Webb would look ridiculously awkward and false, whereas an imaginary lawn mower takes on reality. The audience sees Mr. Webb living, free from any sense of intention for some other end. The convention of pantomime presents the thing itself.

The characters of Grover's Corners appear to possess specific individuality, but Wilder—just as he carefully created a general place with his bare stage and allowed for the audience to glimpse generalized living partly through the pantomime—creates general character types behind the specific Webbs and Gibbses. Gertrude Stein, in *Narration*, explained how the arbitrary, imaginative creation of characters was superior to actual reality: "Vasari and Plutarch are like that, they make them up so completely that if they are not invented, they might as well be they do not really feel that any of the ones about whom they tell had any life except the life they are given by their telling. That can happen and when it does it is writing."[32] Stein observes that the illusion of life rather than reported life is the result of imagination, and illusion possesses an absolute and independent reality. When Wilder converted this idea from narrative prose to stage dialogue, he invented characters who needed the cooperative imagination of the audience for their full vitality. But the characters must be played by actors, of course, and Wilder depended very heavily upon his performers for complete characterization. He wrote:

> Characterization in a novel is presented by the author's dogmatic assertion that the personage was such, and by an analysis of the personage with generally an account of his or her past. Since in the drama this is replaced by the actual presence of the personage before us and since there is no occasion for the intervening all-knowing author to instruct us as to his or her inner nature, a far greater share is given in a play to (1) highly characteristic utterances. . . .

These characteristic utterances, though they are part of all dramatic characterization, are most obvious in comedy: Mrs. Malaprop's misapplication of words in Sheridan's *The Rivals,* for example. The nagging of the children by Mrs. Webb and Mrs. Gibbs more generally characterizes their motherly care ("and (2) concrete occasions in which the character defines itself under action. . . ."). George's tears reveal his sensibility and his goodness ("and (3) a conscious preparation of the text whereby the actor may build upon the suggestions in the rôle according to his own abilities" [*AC*, 119–20]). The last introduces Wilder's dependence upon his actors to make his very general characters specific and actual.

Boleslavsky in his chapter on characterization distinguishes between what the actor must understand from the author's text and what the actor contributes to the play from his own life. The actor is not free to imagine the way his character thinks. The author has already done that; the character exists to reveal the author's ideas. Because "The most powerful weapon of an author is his mind," the actor must "grasp the characterization . . . of the author's mind and follow it."[33] Boleslavsky seems to be suggesting that the actor must understand what the playwright is dramatizing in his play entire and also what his character's part is in the whole. The actor does this by "studying and rehearsing him for a length of time," after which he "ought to know the movement of the author's thoughts." "Try to understand the author,"[34] he says.

Both Wilder and Boleslavsky expect that intelligent study of a play's text, along with rehearsal, will lead the actor to an understanding of what the play is about. Of course, many actors depend upon their director to do this task. When Wilder speaks of the actor building on "the suggestions in the rôle," he does not go on to explain exactly what that means, though he does say that it derives from a "combination of observation, self-knowledge, imagination, and representational skill" (AC, 120). These traits are exactly what Boleslavsky expects from the actor when he speaks of "nature" and "training." Boleslavsky goes on to consider the emotional life of the character: "The emotion of a character is the only sphere where the author should pay attention to the actor's demands and adjust his writings to the actor's interpretation. . . . Emotion is God's breath in a part."[35] Through the contribution of emotion the actor brings the part to life. Wilder said much the same thing when he wrote, "characterization in a play is like a blank check which the dramatist accords to the actor for him to fill in," though as a cautionary word he added that the check is "not entirely blank, for a number of indications of individuality are already there" (AC, 120).

Wilder acknowledges the differences one actor will bring to a role from another. These differences are the actor's contribution to the character's emotional life, and though they definitely are essential to the success of the play—especially in the commercial theater—they do not matter to the play's meaning. Many readers especially, but also viewers of weak productions of Our Town, are disappointed to feel that the characters in the play are not interesting psychologically. This response is correct in that the characters Wilder has written have only the barest individual psychology, but the response is wrong because Wilder never intended his characters to arouse interest in this way.

Though Hollywood is always alert for "properties" to develop, *Our Town,* because it is far removed from realism, seems an unlikely possibility. So much of the play's effectiveness depends upon stage theatricality. Though it was proposed to him, Wilder did not write the script for *Our Town* or for any of the films made from his other works. He was interested in movies and did work for a time after the success of *The Bridge of San Luis Rey* as a scriptwriter. He is credited by many critics for the exceptional success of Alfred Hitchcock's *Shadow of a Doubt,* his only complete script. He understood that movies of plays do not belong to the playwright, but he did offer suggestions for the transfer of his stage ideas to the screen. There quite naturally arose some difficulties over finding ways in the different medium to maintain the meaning of the play. Some of the correspondence between Sol Lesser, the producer, and Wilder has been published, and it is helpful to see what Wilder thought was important to save from his play.

The opening speeches of the Stage Manager presented problems for which no film answer could be found easily. Lesser supported an idea that would lose the Stage Manager's identity in that of Mr. Morgan, the druggist. This was not just a loss of a character; as we shall see, it also lost the important meaning brought about by the pretense of one character "acting" another part. A second way to open the movie that was suggested was to show the Stage Manager with a jigsaw puzzle of the United States. Though this was not used, Wilder wrote in its support, saying that it had an advantage "of setting the background against the whole United States, that constant allusion to larger dimensions of time and place, which is one of the principal elements of the play. . . ."[36] The jigsaw map could have been like the address on Jane Crofut's letter, an invitation to wander, and it is a visual version of American geography that Stein argued was basic to the American's view of himself and reality.

In another letter to Sol Lesser about whether or not Emily should really die at the play's conclusion, Wilder distinguished between the effects on the audience of characters on stage and in the movies: "In a movie you see the people so *close to* that a different relation was established. In a theatre they are halfway abstractions in an allegory; in a movie they are very concrete. So insofar as it's a concrete happening it's not important that she die; it's even disproportionately cruel that she die."[37] Wilder reveals here that he thought of his characters as "halfway abstractions in an allegory," which means that, though he appears to be telling the story of Emily and George, he is actually using them and some incidents from their life to tell the audience something else. Emily and George are interesting only insofar as they illustrate Wilder's ideas. Emily's death in itself is unimportant. The actress who plays Emily must grasp this, but she is free to make Emily as compelling emotionally/psychologically as her gifts as an actress permit. The differences between one actress's understanding of Emily's emotional life and another's are almost totally irrelevant, except when they interfere with Wilder's ideas. This is why Boleslavsky says an actor must understand the playwright's mind but bring his own emotional nature to his characterization. Emily and George as individuals are not the primary interest of Wilder the playwright, though they might interest Wilder the private man. He knew they would interest the audience, too, and he depends on his actors to satisfy that interest, though he will repeatedly interrupt it. Their chief function in *Our Town* is to represent a young woman and a young man and to illustrate an idea of living. So the audience that goes to *Our Town* looking for intimate personal revelation is looking for the wrong thing. Wilder's play was revolutionary beyond its use of the bare stage, and still he is almost alone in making this revolution work in the commercial theater apart from the experimental fringe.

The distinction between the mind of the author portrayed through the characters and the emotions of the characters brought by the actors is vital to any understanding of *Our Town* because it is the mind that Wilder wished to dramatize—and further, the mind free from emotion. Stein helped him to understand this distinction. He wrote to her after reading her book *The Geographical History of America:*

> What a book! I mean What a book! I've been living for a month with ever-increasing intensity of the conceptions of Human Nature and the Human Mind. . . . Those things, yes and identity, have become cell and marrow in me and now at last I have more about them. . . .[38]

Human Nature is that part of characterization that is expressed through the emotions. In the introduction Wilder wrote for Stein's book he said,

> Human Nature clings to identity, its insistence on itself as personality, and to do this it must employ memory and the sense of an

audience. By memory it is reassured of its existence through consciousness of itself in time-succession. By an audience it is reassured
of itself through its effect on another. . . .

(*AC*, 187–88)

Human Nature is comforted by the reassurances of time succession,
one thing following another according to a logical plan based on past
experience, and of audience—here one is reminded of Wilder's com-
ments on G. B. Shaw—but it is also trapped in these reassurances in
order to maintain its identity. And Human Nature is afraid to be separated from them. The emotions are the means by which the self is
asserted, because emotions are reactions of the self or a plea for reactions from others.

The Human Mind, on the other hand, is independent; it has no
identity; every moment "it knows what it knows when it knows it"
(*AC*, 188). The Human Mind is freely acting directly in experience. It
is not reacting or planning its acting: "It gazes at pure existing. It is
deflected by no consideration of an audience, for when it is aware of
an audience it has ceased to know" (*AC*, 188).

Wilder, following Stein, relates these observations to language
and storytelling and religion, which will be considered later. Here it is
important to realize the meaning to Wilder's characterization and acting performance. Wilder wished to portray the Human Mind through
his characters. He called them "the vast multitudes of the world who
[are] striving to escape from the identity-bound and time-immersed
state" (*AC*, 188), and he identified them with being American. What
is at home on the empty stage? In Wilder's kind of theater, the answer
is the Human Mind.

In the first manuscript version of *Our Town,* the Stage Manager
played all the children but Emily and George, Simon Stimson, Mrs.
Forrest, Mr. Morgan, the druggist, and the minister who performs the
wedding. Wilder was sufficiently concerned about the strangeness of
this device to have the Stage Manager tell the audience that he was
now going to play Mr. Morgan in front of his drugstore. This explanation was later removed, and he concluded that having the Stage
Manager assume so many roles was distracting. Wilder left him Mrs.
Forrest's lines, and he played Mr. Morgan easily, while the roles of
Stimson, Rebecca, and Wally were given to actors. What Wilder was
after, however, is clear: the separation of the idea of the human indi-

vidual from the easy realistic means of actually producing him on stage, looking and acting just like himself.

What Wilder chooses to happen on stage helps to determine the characterization. Between the scene of George and the two families on the wedding morning itself, the Stage Manager interrupts with a scene of how it all began:

> George and Emily are going to show you now the conversation they had when they first knew that . . . that . . . as the saying goes . . . they were meant for one another.
>
> (60)

The characters, not the actors, will *show* us, not their feelings (though the actors may do that) but the conversation they had—and this conversation is what they said when they *knew*. What they knew, through some gentle irony at the expense of the cliché "meant for one another," from which Wilder separates himself by the hesitation of the Stage Manager even to say the words, seems less significant than their knowing it.

The Stage Manager asks the audience to remember their feeling when they "were first in love" (60). This takes the task from Wilder of portraying in George and Emily his own intimate perceptions of those feelings. He goes even further in his ironic method of distancing himself from emotion-laden memory when he says about George and Emily's being elected class officers for their senior year in high school, "I don't have to tell you how important that is" (60). It is, of course, important for the moment to those elected, but Wilder dismisses our memories with an ironic smile. The "big thing" in which the Stage Manager expresses interest is something else.

Emily, largely because of act 3, is the single most important character in *Our Town*, except perhaps for the Stage Manager. But act 2 belongs to George, and especially in the scene where "all this began" (60). He motivates all the shifts that move the scene along: he asks to carry Emily's books, he asks Emily about her change in attitude toward him, he suggests the ice cream soda, and he decides to give up further schooling and start directly working on the farm.

After George, probably because he does not perceive it, ignores Emily's rebuff to his request to walk with her and carry her books, he asks her, "Emily, why are you mad at me?" (62). She denies being mad, weakly at first, and then she accuses him of having changed, "spending all your time at *baseball* . . . you've got awful conceited and stuck-up" (62–63). He admits that, through lack of awareness, faults may have crept into his character. Emily insists men should be perfect, after all her and George's fathers are, and then she wishes she had not said it. "Now I can see it's not the truth at all. And I suddenly feel that it isn't important anyway" (64).

Emily is expressing her fear that George is leaving her behind. She already knows, as she tells George later, that she wants George. Emily's behavior is similar, but in a different guise, to that Wilder detected in the letters of another Emily—Emily Dickinson. He wrote that "Its general character is that of archness" (*AC*, 51). He thought that it derived from a girl's relationship with her authoritative father, and therefore he appropriately brought up Emily's idea of the perfectibility of men. We saw Emily testing her father in act 1 with her grand-lady manner, and failing; he thought her comic. Later, during the wedding, Emily expresses her last attempt to persuade and appeal to her father through *"misplaced coquetry"* (*AC*, 51): "Don't you remember that you used to say,—all the time you used to say—all the time: that I was *your* girl! There must be lots of places we can go to. I'll work for you. I could keep your house," (75). But Mr. Webb is a well-balanced father, married to a strong woman; he says, "You mustn't think of such things" (75). And he calls George, telling Emily that George is the "best young fellow in the world" (76). Emily grows up at this moment, leaving her childish flirting with her father behind her.

"Its enactment between daughter and father is a mere harmless dress-rehearsal for later encounters" (*AC*, 51–52). It never works with mothers, and Wilder showed Emily failing to command her mother's admiration for her looks. Wilder recognized that "It is perfectly in order (and *arises from profound natural springs* [my italics]) when it is exhibited by a young woman as a response to a young man who is showing deep interest in her" (*AC*, 51). The girl wishes "to be succeeding and (note the word) winning" (*AC*, 51). And what is the success? What does she win? "Love, attentive love, and the sense of one's identity rebounding from some intelligent and admired being" (*AC*, 52).

In many contexts this infantile archness would be disagreeable. At the soda fountain, just as during the wedding, it is a clue to Emily's fear, and she even repudiates it. It is the expression of her perfectly natural desire for George; she wants to win him and his love, not so much as a prize, but because he represents the object of her desire and her admiration at once. Her uncertainty about him and even about what she wants from him is the source of her coquetry, and when she weeps, she reveals to the audience the genuine positive feeling beneath what appears to be provocative dissimulation.

George is also indirect, though his question about Emily's anger with him, his invitation for an ice cream soda, and his request that she write to him when he's away at State Agricultural College seem straightforward enough. The Stage Manager said we were going to witness the conversation George and Emily had when they *first* knew. This means that they are not in the situation of many stage characters who know what they want, but are revealed while struggling to get it. George and Emily are discovering "they were meant for one another." The audience does not learn what they know. The Stage Manager has told us that already. We will know *that* they know it, and *how* they know it. Emily knows George is the one for her, but she does not know if she will ever be the one for him, which is what he will know when the scene is complete. Everything depends on what George will know, and so the stages of his learning mark the rhythm of the scene.

Through his growing awareness that being away at college could mean growing away from Grover's Corners, having to study more— we have already seen George's limitations as a scholar—and delaying taking over his uncle's farm, George realizes that he will be without Emily. At first he says, "I feel that you're as good a friend as I've got. I don't need to go and meet people in other towns" (67). Then he feels that he's truly "found a person that [he's] very fond of . . . I mean a person who's fond of [me,] too" (68). Finally he asks her, "*could* you be," . . . and he learns "this is an important talk we've been having" (69).

Readers of this scene, though seldom viewers when it is played successfully, sometimes conclude that Emily has maneuvered George and trapped him into marriage. These readers do not heed the Stage Manager's description that we shall see when *they* first knew. George and Emily, as much as Shaw's Tanner and Ann, are seized by life and thrown into each other's arms. It is not possible for any of them "to impose conditions on the irresistible force of Life."[39] Grover's Corners is "the way we were . . . at the beginning of the twentieth century" (32), and George and Emily cannot free themselves from Grover's Corners insofar as it symbolizes living.

George is an American, not Shaw's European, and through George Wilder is showing some of his ideas about the American experience. In his introduction to Gertrude Stein's *Four in America* he attempted to explain a bewildering observation about Americans—that they "cannot earn a living or be a success" (*AC,* 209). This does not mean Americans cannot earn money or "do what they have to do and [even] that they can become 'names which everyone knows'" (*AC,* 209). What it does mean is Americans do not wait or "live in the expectation that circumstance is coming toward them bearing gifts." Nor does the American strain "for the situations he may profit by; he is what he is, and what he *is,* not what he *wills,* is his expression" (*AC,* 210). Wilder's American responds directly in his living to what he is. He does not identify with some future goal, nor does he expect any of his goals to be anything more than they are, that is, he does not expect achievement to make him happy, rich, or famous. The American in his living is committed to the Human Mind, and he rejects Human Nature.

All of George's actions on this spring afternoon are spontaneous responses to what he is at the moment he does them. By doing them he knows what he is: meant for Emily; and what he wants: Emily, too. On this afternoon that is all. There is no actual proposal, for example; he just makes up his mind not to go to college! A proposal of marriage suggests some expectation of something to follow from being meant for one another. And it would demand either some individual psychology and probably either comedy or a swelling of sound from the orchestra and a romantic clinch—all of which Wilder wants to avoid, because such a scene would be either meaningless or sentimental. George is in Wilder's (or Stein's) term, a failure: he fails to propose, he fails to scheme for the success of the farm, and he fails even to imagine what the farm will do for him. George and Emily do, of course, marry, but that is a different event from knowing that they are meant for one another.

Wilder wrote, "An American is insubmissive, lonely, self-educating, and polite. His politeness conceals his slowness to adopt any ideas which he does not feel that he has produced himself" (*AC,* 4). Politeness is the American's response to any authority. He courteously listens, but privately he takes his own counsel. Behind this behavior is a "reluctance to concede that there is an essential truth" (*AC,* 4). If he has to do a thing, he has lost his freedom (*AC,* 8). This is partly the explanation for George's eagerness to learn farming by farming and not by going to school.

He rejects the authority of the Agricultural College and converts the necessity of learning about farming into choosing to learn. "Americans constantly feel that the whole world's thinking has to be done over again. . . . Americans start from scratch (*AC*, 37).

Wilder understood that George's knowing, expressed when he says, "I'm going to make up my mind right now. I won't go" (67), involved loss. He wrote, "Every American is an autodidact. . . . To others this must all seem very deplorable. To Americans it is wearing and costing and often desolating" (*AC*, 38). Wilder only hints at the possibility of George's desolation later in act 3. George has had Emily and his farm, but we see him at the last, fallen full-length at the feet of the dead Emily, when he has lost her who gave meaning to his life through their friendship and love, though, of course, he still has their children and the farm. George's loss is really evidence of how much he has won.

Not going to college will, as Emily points out, make learning to farm harder. She is also aware that he will be limited by the narrowness of Grover's Corners. He will not meet other, new people. He will not have new experiences. He will not enlarge his awareness. He will not outgrow Grover's Corners—or if he does, he will not easily (we remember Simon Stimson) be able to find any activity to use his new knowledge, except marriage. Though he did not enlarge on the "wearing and costing and often desolating" side of George's decision, Wilder represented it fairly.

George and Emily are not expected to compel the interest of the audience by doing unusual things or by revealing a peculiar personality. They exist to dramatize ideas about what it is to be an American, but they are actual. But if the emotions contributed by the actors change from performance to performance and production to production, it does not matter, so long as these emotions do not interfere with the ideas.

Wilder is not writing a metaphysics. He knows that audiences cannot help being interested in the lives and destiny of the characters on stage. Audiences, with the help of good actors, instinctively respond to the plight of the characters; their attention is arrested by the activity taking place on stage. But the story of *Our Town* is really no more interesting in itself than the characters. The story is of American living in act 1, American marriage in act 2, and American dying in act 3. It is, in the chilly phrase from T. S. Eliot's *Sweeney Agonistes*, "Birth and copulation, and death. / That's all. . . ." Wilder knowingly tells a story whose events are pretty much those of every life, but his plotting is full of surprises.

After act 2 establishes the repetitions of the beginning of the first act as well as the differences, it moves easily to the breakfast table of Dr. and Mrs. Gibbs. They naturally discuss George and Emily's wedding, but they contribute remarkably little about the story. They do not discuss events; instead they make observations about weddings and marriages. There is never any question that marriage is a "natural" organization of life, but what George's parents think about marriage is not a rosy picture of bliss.

Children, one of the main purposes of marriage, are a cause of anxiety. The parents worry that George is too young to marry; he will never manage. The relationship between parents and children is painful.

> Dr. Gibbs: . . . I tell you Julia, there's nothing so terrifying in the world as a *son*. The relation of father and son is the darndest, awkwardest—
> Mrs. Gibbs: Well, mother and daughter's no picnic, let me tell you.

Dr. Gibbs concludes, "They'll have a lot of troubles, I suppose, but that's none of our business. Everybody has a right to their own troubles" (52–53). The experienced parents can only offer freedom to their children—freedom to be unhappy in their own way, freedom to live.

Dr. Gibbs, remembering his own wedding day, says he thought Mrs. Gibbs was "the prettiest girl I'd ever seen. . . ." but he adds, "the only trouble was that I'd never seen you before. There I was . . . marryin' a total stranger." And Mrs. Gibbs responds, "weddings are perfectly awful things. Farces,—that's what they are!" (52). Weddings are cruel public acknowledgments that the couple has joined the community.

Dr. Gibbs again remembers, with no more nostalgic comfort than his memory of his bride, that "one of the things I was scared of . . . was . . . we wouldn't have material for conversation more'n'd last us a few weeks." The Gibbses think his fear comic on this morning, and it is, but it is also evidence of his youthful ignorance and silliness, both grotesque and touching. Mrs. Gibbs concludes, "well,—good weather, bad weather—'tain't very choice, but I always find something to say" (53). The evidence of the subject and quality of her conversation does not even allow the audience to believe the pun on the weather—she keeps on talking in all weather, if only about the weather—is the product of her own wit.

George appears, making a rote joke about his marriage being suicide, and goes to visit the Webbs, where he is prevented from seeing Emily by the superstition that "the groom can't see his bride on his wedding day, not until he sees her in church" (55). Here and in the wedding scene Wilder insists on the traditional and customary aspects of weddings to put this wedding in the context of repetition and millions of other weddings. In the light of Dr. Gibbs and Mrs. Gibbs's conversation and of George's and Emily's thoughts at the wedding later, this particular superstition seems to have a common-sensical practical purpose. If the bride and groom did actually see each other privately, they might call the whole thing off: "A girl's apt to be a mite nervous on her wedding day" (57).

George protests to his future father-in-law, "I wish a fellow could get married without all that marching up and down." Mr. Webb's answer sounds like the clichéd explanation for the conflict between restraint and freedom based on sexual difference: "Every man that's ever lived has felt that way about it. . . . It's the womenfolk who've built up weddings. . . . For a while now the women have it all their own. A man looks pretty small at a wedding. . . . All those good women standing shoulder to shoulder making sure that the knot's tied in a mighty public way" (57).

Wilder lets the "opposition" explain—with some irony—the value of tying the knot so publicly. The women are standing shoulder to shoulder to ensure that men will maintain their commitment to the idea of the family, that they will keep their promise. When they say, "I plight my troth," they pledge their truth so publicly, that reneging would be difficult. The keeping is as important as the promise because the idea of the family depends on it. George hears only the ironic tone of Mr. Webb's speech. He asks anxiously, "you *believe* in it, don't you, Mr. Webb?" Webb reassures him, "Marriage is a wonderful thing" (57), but Webb's word choice allows for an ambiguous meaning, which Webb does not clarify.

Webb almost tells George about something that is more important than age as a basis for beginning a successful marriage, but he catches himself and stops. Each member of the audience can imagine for himself what those "other things" might be. Because Wilder, through Webb, does not commit himself to any limited definition of marriage, each individual in the audience is forced to contribute his own experience and judgment to defining the idea of marriage. Marriage is an ordinary enough institution, but each marriage is different from all the others, and no definition could satisfy everybody.

Webb does pass on to George some advice he had from his father: ". . . start out early showing who's boss . . . give an order, even if it don't make sense; just so she'll learn to obey. . . . if anything about your wife irritates you . . . just get up and leave the house. . . . never, *never* let your wife know how much money you have, never." He adds, "So I took the opposite of my father's advice and I've been happy ever since" (58). Mr. Webb's father's advice is lunatic and comic, but that does not mean that millions of husbands have not behaved exactly like that. The uniqueness of each marriage is stressed; the experience of others in the past is no help. Wilder's American is "self-educating." There is no "essential truth." "For Americans there is no inherent and essential authority accruing to [fathers or to] the elderly, either" (*AC*, 4). Neither Wilder nor Webb attempts to offer any specific definition of a good marriage.

With relief Webb turns to the subject of raising chickens. "There is only one way in which an American can feel himself in relation to other Americans—when he is united with them in a project" (*AC*, 16). Mr. Webb can feel comfortable with George and like him as an individual—not in his function of son-in-law—but when they can talk together about his enthusiasm for experimenting with the "Philo System of raising chickens" in an incubator. Mrs. Webb, who does not share her husband's enthusiasm for his plans, has heard them more often than she can bear. Because she is a woman, and more practically concerned about Emily's future as a wife, she wishes irritatedly that "you two'd be talking about things worth while" (59). Webb *"bitingly"* replies that he will leave her to give George good advice.

No wonder George returns home *"bewildered and crestfallen"* (59). Or that Webb tells Mrs. Webb of that superstition older than the one that prevents the groom from seeing the bride until the ceremony: "Since the cave men: no bridegroom should see his father-in-law on the day of the wedding, or near it" (60). Fathers and sons, mothers and daughters, fathers-in-law and sons-in-law—the scene establishes a fundamental difficulty in each relationship. There is the traditional irritation between generations. But this scene is specifically about marriage. The experienced parents feel helpless in the face of the difficulties they know are waiting in the future. They can prevent neither the marriage nor its troubles. The children yearn for some reassurance their parents cannot confidently provide. Parents and children are each on opposite sides of an unbridgeable gulf. Only when the children have been married can they understand their parents. Then it is too late. Careful examination of this scene reveals that Wilder says scarcely one thing in favor of marriage, except that it satisfies essential demands of nature, and he says a great many negative things. The view that Wilder's picture of life is naively optimistic is not supported by the text of the play.

Both the Gibbses and Webbs are put out of humor, Rebecca is upstairs crying, and George is dismayed. The Stage Manager interrupts, though he is not entirely comforting: "You know how it is: you're twenty-one or twenty-two and you make some decisions; then whissh'—you're seventy." The condition of young love when the decisions are made is "like a person sleepwalking. . . . You're just a little bit crazy" (60). Still the interruption introduces the scene when George and Emily first know "they are meant for one another," and their innocent hope is a relief from the frustration of the wedding morning.

In the theater of 1938, the jump from the wedding morning to an earlier time, the time before George and Emily knew they would marry, was unusual and startling on the stage. Flashbacks had long been a part of the technique of fiction, and they were as frequently used then as now in the movies, but they were unexpected on the stage. Wilder intended his flashback to provide interest for his audience, and he knew it provided a break from the usual progression of time on the stage, but more important to him was its function of reinforcing the play's meaning. The switch to an earlier time is like the jumps to the future in act 1: the deaths of some of the characters, the imminence of the automobile, World War I. The technique calls into question the uncertainty of the time of anything we are seeing on the stage. It is an attempt to suggest that these events are taking place all at the same time everywhere. The audience is seeing one such isolated incident, but the activity is not unique. The progression—proposal, wedding morning, wedding—is the usual one, but it has little meaning apart from the expected sequence of cause and effect, one thing following another. Wilder's arrangement stresses something different. His sequence is the idea of the inevitability and also the difficulty of marriage, and then of how big things like planning to spend a lifetime together begin, and then of the confusion in people's minds that underlies the orderly ceremony of the wedding. The events are shown in a surprising sequence. The audience is never allowed the satisfaction of witnessing a completed and resolved event. George does not get to see Emily on their wedding morning. He never really proposes. The wedding is repeatedly interrupted. Instead of story, the audience gets parts of a story that force attention on meaning.

Wilder wrote in "Some Thoughts on Playwriting": "The dramatist through working in the theater gradually . . . learns, above all, to organize the play in such a way that its strength lies not in appearances beyond his control, but in the succession of events and in the unfolding of an idea, in narration" (*AC*, 117). He added:

> the theater carries the art of narration to a higher power than the novel or the epic poem. The theater is unfolding action and in the disposition of events the authors may exercise a governance so complete that the distortions effected by the physical appearance of actors, by the fancies of scene-painters and the misunderstandings of directors, fall into relative insignificance. It is just because the theater is an art of many collaborators, with the constant danger of grave misinterpretation, that the dramatist learns to turn his attention to the laws of narration, its logic, and its deep necessity of presenting a unifying idea stronger than its mere collection of happenings. The dramatist must be by instinct a story teller.
>
> (*AC*, 117–18)

Events in themselves have small significance simply because they might have happened. The playwright depends on the arrangement of events, which he can control, to convey his idea. The playwright organizes the events into a plot that tells his story and at the same time presents a strong unifying idea. This idea can survive even the distortions and misinterpretations of those people who are responsible for a production of the play, and over whom the playwright has little or no control.

When Wilder wrote of the "laws of narration," he had in mind Gertrude Stein's observations in her book *Narration*. She wrote, "Narrative has been the telling of anything because there has been always has been a feeling that something that something followed another thing that there was succession in happening."[40] Narrative in the past was recounting what took place. It followed a pattern in time. One thing followed another. Cause and effect were assumed or imposed. Obviously the writer selected from among all the things that happened to report only those things that contributed to his idea. The past could be introduced into the present. That is, what had happened could be related by someone, thus mixing past and present times. This method works very well in the theater, where a character describes what has happened.

It is unfortunate that Wilder used Gertrude Stein's word *succession* to mean something different from her use. He meant simply the following of one thing after another in the work—the novel or the play or the poem. She meant the imitation in a work of the way one thing follows another in time or in simple logical explanation.

The scene with George and Emily after school at the soda fountain follows the scene of the wedding morning. But the soda fountain scene does not follow the wedding morning in time. And it does not explain the wedding morning. If George is marrying Emily, the audience already knows that he must have decided to marry her. These scenes follow one after the other to develop an idea. Wedding morning: the idea of marriage. Soda fountain: what young people know when they know they want to marry. Gertrude Stein wrote that now, "everything is not that thing there is at present not a sense of anything being successively happening, moving is in every direction beginning and ending is not really exciting, anything is anything, any thing is happening and anybody can know anything at any time that anything is happening and so . . . is there now any narrative of any successive thing."

The consequences of planning a plot where "moving is in every direction" is to change the definition of beginning. Event does not begin; meaning does. Act 1 of *Our Town* does not begin with the birth of any of the characters, though there is the birth of the twins. The day begins, but it does again in each of the other two acts, too. There is no beginning event to the story at all. Wilder begins at the beginning of his idea about life in the twentieth (or perhaps every other) century.

Stein continued her explanation, "gradually well if you are an American gradually you find that really it is not necessary not really necessary that anything that everything has a beginning and middle and an ending and so you are struggling with anything as anything has begun and began does not really mean that thing does not really mean beginning or begun. . . . [41] She distinguishes here between the meaning of an event because of its place in a time sequence and its actual value or its emotional value. This distinction is important to Wilder; *Our Town* has a story, but it focuses more on its abstract meaning than on reporting its succession of events in time. So we get glimpses of the story of the Gibbses and the Webbs, but those glimpses are arranged in such a way as to tell a different story.

Using the Old Testament as a model of "permanently good reading" because there is no time/event succession, Stein observed, "So then in the Old Testament writing there is really no actual conclusion that anything is progressing that one thing is succeeding another thing, that anything in that sense in the sense of succeeding happening is a narrative of anything."[42] The moving is in all directions, without beginning, middle, and ending. "There is really no actual conclusion." As she said before, "ending is not really exciting." In the Old Testament, temporal and geographical locations derive their importance from their relation to God. In the Old Testament this is possible because of the claim to absolute authority that God and his account possess. The story has no beginning or ending because God is without beginning and ending, and the human characters function as evidence of the continuing story. There is a constant projection into the promise of the future. This is exactly the effect Wilder hoped to achieve. He set his play in the past, partly at least, so that the audience could feel itself continuing the life it saw on stage. The audience represented the future of the characters in the play, but it was also in the same situation as the characters in the play in being a living past for people yet to come.

Our Town is a series of glimpses of life, each without beginning or ending, in the sense of cause and finality. The life is continuing. And the life, for all the specific detail of heliotrope and algebra, is an abstract idea, almost one of biological necessity, of the continuing advance of the human creature. The events are important only as they dramatize the idea. As events interesting for themselves, nothing happens. As events meaning something else, everything that needs to happen to maintain life happens. People are born, they mature, they marry, they have children, and they die.

The wedding dramatizes everybody's having some place on a continuum, with a past—"the ancestors. Millions of them"—and a future—"The real hero of this scene [who] isn't on the stage at all" (71). That is the Stage Manager's sermon, and Wilder's sermon, too.

Most people like wedding ceremonies. They take pleasure in the ceremony and are curious about the participants. But wedding ceremonies on stage are not interesting, because the stage is already a kind of ceremony, and a ceremony of a ceremony is lifeless. In theatrical representations of weddings drama is created by having something go wrong. The struggle between the characters and the ceremonial order imposed on them produces dramatic conflict. We all remember plays and movies and novels where the wedding is interrupted, say, by a man who should or thinks he should be the groom. Shakespeare's *Much Ado About Nothing* or Cervantes's story of Fernando and Luscinda in *Don Quixote* are among the most famous and best loved. Wilder worried about the transfer of his wedding to the movies. In the letter to Sol Lesser, he reveals that he was aware of exactly what he had accomplished in the staging of the wedding:

> My only worry is that—realistically done—your wedding scene won't be interesting enough, and that it will reduce many of the surrounding scenes to ordinaryness. . . .
>
> On the stage with *Our Town* the novelty was supplied by
>
> (1) economy of effect in scenery.
> (2) the minister was played by the Stage Manager.
> (3) the thinking-aloud passages.
> (4) the oddity of hearing Mrs. Soames' gabble during the ceremony.
> (5) the young people's movements of alarm. . . .
> —And for a story that is so generalized [the danger of dwindling to the conventional] . . . is great.
> The play interested because every few minutes there was a new bold effect in presentation-methods. . . .[43]

The story is a generalized one. It was never intended by Wilder to supply the major interest in the play. Neither was a realistic presentation of turn-of-the-century small-town New England. The nostalgia so many claim to find in the play is probably something they bring to it.

I have already examined some of the effects of the bare stage and the Stage Manager's assumption of roles in the play. Number 3 on Wilder's list, "the thinking-aloud passages," is used only during the wedding, though something like them is spoken by Emily in her return to her twelfth birthday. Mrs. Webb starts, and her speech is not a soliloquy. She "speaks to the audience." The Stage Manager and other characters in act 1 have addressed the audience; although this is the first time silent thinking is dramatized, the audience is prepared for Mrs. Webb's speech to them. She, in turn, by marking a small change, prepares for George's strange behavior, and finally for Emily's brief but violent thoughts about marriage addressed to no-one at all. The choir is singing throughout, supplying the order of the ceremony, which never takes place. They are soothing and reassuring, but the singing is also the force against which George and Emily struggle. It is the voice of all those ancestors, encouraging but also bullying. "Why's everybody pushing me so?" (73). The meaning of "the thinking-aloud passages" here is not very different from those of act 1 or act 3, as we shall see, but the dramatic function has changed.

George's fears about marriage are not expressed by thinking aloud. He speaks to his mother about his fear of growing old. He is not ready to give up being a baseball-playing youth to assume the burden of manhood. Only when he thinks of Emily, the particular woman apart from the generalized situation, does he come to himself. He does want her—as we have seen when he decides at the soda fountain not to go to college.

Emily feels alone and speaks to herself. When she sees George, she hates him and wishes she were dead. Emily, like all those "good women standing shoulder to shoulder," needs to be reminded of the promise: "Emily, I'm going to do my best. I love you, Emily. I need you." She answers his promise and his need with her own need: "Well, if you love me, help me. All I want is someone to love me. . . . And I mean for *ever*. Do you hear? For ever and ever" (76). Her "for ever" is a demand from George, but it is also a promise that she will want his love always, too. Wilder knows as well as anyone that such promises can be broken, but human beings must have some faith in them to keep on making them.

When the Stage Manager says a few words from the wedding ceremony, the attention of the audience is arrested by Mrs. Soames's gabble about the loveliness of the wedding and her crying at weddings because she likes to see young people happy. George and Emily are not precisely a happy couple, though they are an expression of hopeful possibility.

The Stage Manager asks, "Do I believe in it?" and answers, "I don't know." His description of married life is not encouraging: "The cottage, the go-cart, the Sunday-afternoon drives in the Ford, the first rheumatism, the grandchildren, the second rheumatism, the deathbed, the reading of the will. . . ." (78). But then he acknowledges the audience and smiles: "Once in a thousand times it's interesting." That one marriage, advancing human awareness, makes the human adventure worth it.

Mrs. Soames has the last word. "I always say: *happiness*, that's the great thing! The important thing is to be happy" (78). Perhaps Wilder risked too much in Mrs. Soames. He certainly does not want to leave the audience gloomy about the difficulty of marriage. But just as certainly, that is the view he presents. Mrs. Soames in the first act is not an entirely sympathetic woman because of her petty malice directed against Simon Stimson and her superiority about her husband's irritability. Her silliness at the wedding is not endearing either, not least because she may speak for many in the audience. Happiness, in Wilder's view, may be a "great thing," so great as to count for little as the goal of life. Her giving voice to the idea of happiness relieves a bit the cynicism of the Stage Manager, but dramatically it calls happiness into question. At best happiness seems to be irrelevant to the general scheme of things, but it is also a gift some people receive. Those who are not lucky enough to have it are not necessarily miserable. Wilder has it two ways with happiness. He is not against it, but it does not appear to be a sensible goal or a necessity. It is like the "marching up and down." He gives it its due and calls it into question, too. Happiness is never really dramatized. And neither happiness nor marching up and down is the *important* thing. Being interesting is.

6

Something Eternal

Imaginative narration—the invention of souls and destinies—is to a philosopher an all but indefensible activity.

Its justification lies in the fact that the communication of ideas from one mind to another inevitably reaches the point where exposition passes into illustration, into parable, metaphor, allegory, and myth.

(AC, 125–26)

According to Wilder, a philosopher can justify inventing human beings and their stories only if the activity illustrates ideas. But then it is the business of philosophy in its search for wisdom to focus on the reality of values, not to be distracted by the pleasure of stories. Saint Augustine was dismayed at his own as well as the other spectators' intense emotional response to the invented disasters that took place in the theater of Carthage. And almost everybody knows that Plato was suspicious of poets. Part of the business of a writer, however, is making fictions and fantasies that have an authority of their own. Wilder recounts Gertrude Stein's conclusion about "the spell cast by novelists, the novelist Henry James. . . . 'Novels are true.'" She thought that fiction persuaded the reader to submit to it. It is one of the "irrational ways we have of knowing things, of believing things, and of being governed by these ways of believing" (*AC*, 207).

Wilder's list of narrative forms, beginning with illustration, ends with myth. It is tempting to think of this list as a series of progressive stages in the forms that communication of ideas takes. Wilder had always been interested in myth. In his essay on James Joyce he asked a rhetorical question: "Now, how would we present any individual . . . existing and somehow related to totality?" (*AC*, 176). This is another version of the problem Wilder set for himself in *Our Town*: "I wished to record a village's life on the stage, with realism and with generality" (101). His answer was:

> First we would seek for our place in myths. Myths are the dreaming soul of the race, telling its story. Now, the dreaming soul of the race has told its story for centuries and centuries. . . . They're still telling them. Every novel for sale in a railway station is the dreaming soul of the human race telling its story. . . . The retelling of them on every hand occurs because they whisper a validation . . . and confer a significance.
>
> (*AC*, 176–77)

In his introduction to *Jacob's Dream* by the Austrian playwright Richard Beer-Hofmann, Wilder said that the persistent elements of myth

> are questions and not answers in regard to the human situation. In the majority of cases the questions seem to have to do with the mind disengaging itself from the passions or finding its true position in the presence of the established authorities, human or divine. They are concretizations of man's besetting preoccupation with the mind and the mind's struggle to know itself; and each retelling requires that some answer be furnished to the question that infuses every part of the story.
>
> (*AC*, 129)

The questions contained in a myth are the activities of Stein's Human Mind discovering itself and separating itself from Human Nature. The characters of *Our Town*, especially Emily in act 3 when she returns from the dead, are doing just that. They represent a dramatized struggling to know, to know what is eternal in themselves.

Wilder has always used a kind of myth for the story his plays tell. *The Trumpet Shall Sound,* his first play, is an updated illustration of New Testament texts, an allegory of a householder who returns after an absence to consider the trust of his servants. He had already told the story of Emily's return in his novel *The Woman of Andros,* set in Hellenistic Greece. It is recounted by the Andrian, Chrysis, as though it were a myth, to illustrate the value of life.

This "myth" that is retold in *Our Town* Wilder reshaped then from his earlier telling, but it was also influenced by some of his other work. The portals through which the characters enter and exit in *The Long Christmas Dinner* enclose all human experience and therefore denote birth and death—a main concern in *Our Town.* The woman who dies in *Pullman Car Hiawatha* says farewell to the world much as Emily does. The three-minute play from *The Angel That Troubled the Waters, And the Sea Shall Give Up Its Dead,* pictures the characters "slowly liberating [their] . . . mind from the prides and prejudices and trivialities of a lifetime."[44] These characters are an early version of the dead in the cemetery at Grover's Corners whose job is to forget their earthly lives. Wilder tirelessly worked and reworked the same themes, even after *Our Town.* In *Sloth,* a one-act play from a series *The Seven Deadly Sins,* which Wilder continued to work on until his death, a Mr. Hawkins watches his wife and daughter sewing from outside through a window, recognizes what a treasure life is, and decides to rejoin them. Wilder was struck by the idea of the overwhelming value of life itself apart from any outside authority in the passage in book ll of the *Odyssey,* where Achilleus in the Underworld tells Odysseus that he would rather be living, although a poorly fed slave, pushing a plow, than a king over all the dead.

When Emily joins the dead, the choir is again singing "Blessed Be the Tie That Binds." The hymn in act 1 "bound" all the characters together. In act 2, it bound George and Emily together, and also bound them to the human community as they joined the long march of biology. Now in act 3 it binds Emily, and all of us, to all those millions who have gone before, the dead. And because Mr. Webb remembered it was Emily's favorite hymn, Wilder provides a realistic explanation for its being sung, too. Emily informs Mrs. Gibbs, who is among the dead, about how she and George bought a drinking fountain for the stock on the farm with the three-hundred-and-fifty-dollar legacy she left them. This legacy is, the audience remembers, the money that was to take Mr. and Mrs. Gibbs to France. Emily is proud of the farm and of their new Ford. But Mrs. Gibbs does not seem very interested, and Emily herself becomes aware of some barrier between herself and the concerns of the living. "Live people don't understand, do they? . . . how in the dark live persons are" (89–90).

Wilder has said that the idea of the dead waiting patiently but not without expectation was suggested to him by Dante's portrayal of the Valley of the Repentant Kings in cantos 8 and 9 of the *Purgatorio*. Some of the detail, too, of the scene seems to have been suggested by these two extraordinary cantos. Canto 8 opens with a powerful psychological light, which T. S. Eliot also used in *The Waste Land*, and Byron in *Don Juan:*

> It was now the hour that turns back the desires
>> of seafarers and softens the heart
>> on that day they have said good-bye to sweet friends
> and that stings the new pilgrim
>> with love, if he hears from far away a bell
>> that seems a lament for the dying day.
>
> (8.1–6)

Wilder presents the same combination of delight and melancholy longing in Emily's farewell to the world and arrival in a new scene. In canto 9 Dante enters Purgatory proper with a wonder much like Emily's, and he is warned not to look back, a warning Emily does not heed because she cannot understand it until she returns to the living. Dante focuses his avid attention on the sky, and especially on the stars. Wilder's dead do, too. The Stage Manager says, with some humor, about everybody on *this* star, the Earth, "The strain's so bad [the strain of the earth to make something of itself] that every sixteen hours everybody lies down and gets a rest." And then he dismisses the audience, wishing its members "a good rest, too" (103). Dante reports of himself, "I, who had somewhat of Adam in me, / overcome by sleep, lay down on the grass" (9.10–11). Adam is an image of death, but the overriding sense is of sleep. In an early version of act 3 the dead are visited by some mysterious presence that is a pleasure and comfort to them. So in Dante

> I saw that noble army
>> silently gaze upward
>> as though in expectation, pale and humble,

and I saw two angels come out from above
and descend. . . .

(8.22–26)

The angels would not be appropriate either to the Protestant Americans of Grover's Corners or to Wilder's realistic surface, but the sense of Dante is the same as in the early version of the play. Wilder felt that it was better to drop the windlike presences altogether, but he retained the feeling.

Wilder also has caught Dante's wistful attachment on the part of the dead for the living, despite their separation. Nino Visconti asks Dante to ask his daughter for her prayers.

when you are beyond the wide waters,
tell my Giovanna to call for me
there where the innocent are answered.

(8.70–72)

He says about his wife,

I do not think that her mother loves me any more. . . .
Through her may easily enough be understood
just how long the fire of love lasts in woman
if the eye or touch does not often rekindle it.

(8.73–78)

Dante's description of himself at the conclusion of canto 9 is the intermittent human understanding Wilder has dramatized in act 3.

That exact impression was given to me
by what I was hearing, as we usually get
when people are singing with an organ:
now the words are clear and now are not.

(9.142–45)

Emily wants to return to "the day I first knew that I loved George" (91). That may be the day we saw in act 2, though that day more clearly is the day *George* knew. Emily told George then, "I always have been." *What* Emily has always been is left up in the air, but everybody knows. Emily asks why such a happy day should be painful. The Stage Manager answers, "You not only live it; but you watch yourself living it. . . . And as you watch it, you see the thing that they—down there—never know. You see the future" (91–92). Emily still does not see why it should be painful. Her life after marrying George was a good one, though like all life it ended in death. Finally she is persuaded to choose an unimportant day—her twelfth birthday. The importance to Western civilization of age twelve to fourteen as the time when young men and women are on the edge of the change from child to adult is part of the idea that runs throughout the third act, of transformation from one condition to another, from ignorance to knowledge.

The daily routine that started acts 1 and 2 appears once again. Howie Newsome, Constable Warren, Joe Crowell, Wally, some, if not all the dead, are alive and active. The perspective of death gives the repeating of the morning its emotional power. Emily sees the town she knew as a little girl, before the changes; "it's 1899. This is fourteen years ago" (93). Two years earlier than act 2. The ages of George and Emily do not quite work out. She is twelve in 1899, but about sixteen in 1901. Emily has forgotten some things: the "old white fence that used to be around our house" (93), that "Mama was ever that young" (95), that George had given her a postcard album for her birthday.

The living as well as the dead forget. The dead, in fact, are not any more dead than the dead in Dante's *Purgatorio*. The *Purgatorio* "explores," in Francis Fergusson's words, "the psyche itself—not in terms of its supernatural goal, but in terms of its earthly existence."[45] And Fergusson describes the effect of the early part of the *Purgatorio* that Wilder is making his own as "the poetry of our most primitive awareness of the earthly scene."[46] In considering whether or not Emily should die in the movie version, Wilder wrote to Sol Lesser that it was "disproportionately cruel that she die."[47] Wilder understood the powerful reality of movies and that a movie version of his play would overwhelm the audience with the emphasis on Emily's actual death. The dying was not important; the "poetry" of her "primitive awareness of the earthly scene" is emphasized on her return to her twelfth birthday. That perspective was achieved in the movie by a kind of dream-death, and then Emily wakes and returns to life.

It cannot be stressed sufficiently, because so many misunderstand, that Wilder is neither speculating "about the conditions of life after death" (xi–xii) nor preaching some fatuous philosophy about how to live a fulfilling life. He said:

It is an attempt to find a value above all price for the smallest events in our daily life. I have made the claim as preposterous as possible, for I have set the village against the largest dimensions of time and place. . . . Each individual's assertion to an absolute reality can only be inner, very inner. . . . Our claim, our hope, our despair are in the mind—not in things. . . .

(xii–xiii)

His attention, like Dante's, is directed to the earthly scene. He is dramatizing his view of how we actually live, but he makes his presentation "preposterous" to give it force and clarity. The white fence and the postcard album are not important in themselves. Things in themselves are without power and value.

Emily, who sees herself living her ordinary day, cries to her mother, *"Let's look at one another"* (99). When her mother continues her daily routine, Emily *"breaks down sobbing."* "We don't have time to look at one another. . . . I didn't realize. So all that was going on and we never noticed" (100). Not only has Wilder shown us Emily's awareness from the perspective of the dead that, "Oh, earth, you're too wonderful for anybody to realize you" (100), but he has also filled in the details of the daily living of the Webbs with significance for us. The postcard album is, after all, only a book that would bore us. Its value is generated through Emily's and George's relation to it. It meant something to them. And its power to reveal how inadequate we are in our awareness of our living is partly because it is so small and fragile— forgotten.

Emily is pleading for the importance of "the smallest events of our daily life," not so much that they should be remembered as that they should be noticed and that their inner relationship in the mind should be accounted for. Wilder knows very well that no one can do this every minute, except "The Saints and poets." And he qualifies even this exception—"maybe—they do some" (100). He wrote that Gertrude Stein said to him once:

Everyone when they are young has a little bit of genius, that is they really do listen. They can listen and talk at the same time. Then they grow a little older and many of them get tired and they listen less and less. But some, a very few continue to listen. And finally

they get very old and they do not listen any more. That is very sad;
let us not talk about that.

(AC, 221)

Emily says good-bye to things as well as to experiences: "Good-bye,
Grover's Corners . . . Mama and Papa. Good-bye to clocks ticking . . .
and Mama's sunflowers. And food and coffee. And new-ironed dresses
and hot baths . . . and sleeping and waking up" (100). But the things
are valued only in terms of the effect they produce. Although Wilder
is not preaching for a spiritual reformation, he is reminding the audience of how precious daily life is, because it determines our true reality, how we do our living, how we think our thinking—our Human
Mind. But, and this distinction *must be* repeatedly emphasized, our
enduring identity is not derived from the things and the events because
they are familiar and repeated, but from our ever-new, ever-fresh relation to them. That is what we know—even as we forget the things
and the events, and the people, too. There is no bolstering comfort in
what surrounds us, but there can be an excitement from seeing everything as if for the first time.

Simon Stimson's angry denunciation of life is an affirmation of its
power: "Now you know! That's what it was to be alive. To move
about in a cloud of ignorance; to go up and down trampling on the
feelings of those . . . of those about you. To spend and waste time as
though you had a million years. To be always at the mercy of one self-
centered passion, or another. . . . Ignorance and blindness." Stimson
is right, but Mrs. Gibbs protests, "that ain't the whole truth and you
know it" (101). She is right, too; Stimson's negative awareness of living is partial. But behind his anger is a validation of Emily's return to
the living. Her conclusion is not much different from Stimson's.
"That's all human beings are! Just blind people" (101). Stimson is attached to living through his angry hatred as much as most of us are
attached, "maybe," "some," through wonder. His outburst is witness
to the power of life, in his case, its power to disappoint but not completely destroy expectation. Like Emily, the audience should see breakfast at the Webbs as though they had never seen it before. It is painful
in its newness, and in its beauty. Wilder is convinced the American
hangs on to life, not by clinging to the event but by trying to know his
relation to the event and by greeting as many subsequent events as
possible with the same freshy intensity. Wilder's American struggles to
keep the door open to experience. To live in the ever present now with
awareness.

Emily *does* say good-bye to the delights of the world. It is a recognition and an acceptance that things are lost in the passing of time. Not just sunflowers, but Mama and Papa, too. And all of Grover's Corners. They are gone in the play, and they are gone in our lives, too.

Emily's return and her speech almost unfailingly move audiences. I remember how as a student I was startled to see an entire class weep in response to the reading aloud of some of the speeches and stage directions from this scene. A classroom is not an ideal context for effective theater. But the scene worked even there.

The sense of loss is not primarily because Emily is dead, and we will all die, though death is sad. But death is, after all, a commonplace. And the loss is not because the small events of living are unremembered, gone forever. And not even because we are all inadequate in our living, though our inadequacy is melancholy enough. The audience feels bereft because it is right that Emily say farewell and that the dead forget.

Wilder quoted Gertrude Stein on the necessity of dying.

> If nobody had to die how would there be room enough for any of us who now live to have lived. We never could have been if all the others had not died. There would have been no room.
>
> Now the relation of human nature to the human mind is this.
> Human nature does not know this. . . .
> But the human mind can. . . .
>
> (*AC*, 189)

Human Nature because it clings to survival through the agency of things and orderly repetition rejects the disappearance of the familiar and makes every effort to maintain it. The Human Mind can accept "a non-self situation . . . as an objective fact of experience" (*AC*, 189). This is a painful possibility. Wilder wrote that, "It is not without 'tears' that Human Nature is found to be uninteresting and through a gradual revelation is discovered to be sharing most of its dignities with dogs" (*AC*, 190). Human Nature like the animals lacks the virtue that makes knowing possible.

In *Four in America* Stein conceives a novelist, George Washington. He is not a novelist, according to Wilder, because he invented his life or stood apart from it. A "novelist" governs his inner life. This inner life, that Wilder following Stein identifies with the American experience, is objective because it is based on experience, and it may not be falsified. George Washington the novelist was "disattached from the concrete and the specific. He could and did love concrete things. ('He was charmed with the dresses of the little baby. . . .')." This love "tended to transmute its experiences from things of human nature to things of the human mind" (*AC*, 220). Like Emily, George Washington loves baby dresses (or sunflowers), but though their value includes the direct sensuous experience of them, their enduring value derives from the effort to understand one's relation to them. This struggle of the Human Mind to know is sad then because it involves a deliberate alienation from the world. What Emily sees is not that everybody is inadequate to life as a physical experience, but that through inertia, exhaustion, and distraction, most people cannot understand anything beyond their physical living. And if any should see what Emily sees, there is no inevitable reward, except possibly loneliness. Wilder wrote about another Emily—Emily Dickinson—that she solved the "problem in a way which is of importance to every American: by loving the particular while living in the universal" (*AC*, 63). We are not Emily Dickinson, nor Gertrude Stein, nor George Washington the novelist, and Wilder is not vain or preaching. He is describing what he sees in American life. Not many more in the audience of *Our Town* have recognized exactly what Wilder was dramatizing than have recognized what Gertrude Stein was telling. But audiences did go and do go to see *Our Town,* and they feel Emily's pain and understand that her farewell is fitting.

Emily Dickinson was one of the poets, and perhaps even a saint, that the Stage Manager allowed might realize life as they lived it. George Gibbs is no such creature, and it would be cruel of Wilder to expect him to respond to Emily's death without grief. He returns to the cemetery after the funeral while the dead are discussing the stars and the *millions of years* it took for their light to reach earth. George *"sinks to his knees then falls full length at Emily's feet"* (102). Some of the dead are offended by the impropriety of George's behavior: "That ain't no way to behave!" (102). And Emily says to George's mother, "They don't understand, do they?" (103). From the position of the dead and millions of years, they are right, but "that ain't the whole truth." George will one day, perhaps even before he dies, understand Emily's death from the perspective of the dead. And his grief is like Stein's tears, evidence of the powerful, but temporary claim of Human Nature. But it is equally evidence that the activities of Human

Nature must have a meaning more than creature comfort. Emily, as we saw in act 2, was the reason for George's life. Wilder dramatized him knowing himself when he knew he wanted Emily.

Mrs. Soames says, "My, wasn't life awful—and wonderful" (86). This is a cliché that no one has any trouble with. Its importance in the play is as another, perhaps more obvious, expression of Wilder's paradoxical vision. Wilder accepts the paradoxes: the one and the many, Human Nature and the Human Mind, concrete and abstract, difficulty of marriage and its inevitable desirability, the birth of a child and the death of a mother. But even the paradoxes are not Wilder's principal dramatic interest. It is the separation of the one thing from the other, that gap between *awful* and *wonderful* in life.

There is always separation in the theater. The audience is separated from the action by the proscenium and the curtain; they witness the event, but they do not participate in it directly. Wilder plays with this separation by having his stage be frankly a stage. There is no curtain and no scenery. There is an acknowledgment that the illusion is just that, an illusion. No pretense that the scene on stage is real. At the same time there are actors planted in the audience who talk to the characters on the stage, creating an interaction across the proscenium. These devices bridge the separation between audience and stage, but by constructing a bridge, they call attention to the separation.

As I have tried to suggest in the discussion on acting style, Wilder's play insists upon a separation between the actor and the character. The stage Manager openly assumes other roles. The actors' mime emphasizes the presentational rather than the representational kind of acting. The actor is often deliberately playing the character; at the same time this is done so convincingly that the power of the theater to command belief is successful.

Wilder repeatedly confuses time. He insists on the pastness of the events. The time is the turn of the century. Within the play itself, past time is called up, as with George and Emily in the drugstore *after* the wedding morning. Facts from the future are provided: the death of characters, the coming automobile. Yet as Wilder knew, stage time is always present time: "On the stage it is always now. . . . *A play is what takes place. . . .* A play visibly represents pure existing" (AC, 125). Though the time of the audience is different from the stage time, it is present time, too. Sometimes there is a kind of syncopation between the present time of the audience and that of the play. The audience is aware that it is spending two-and-one-half hours in a theater, but it is watching a story happen that takes many years. And it is helpless in front of that story. All an audience can do is watch and listen to a play. The audience cannot even interfere with the play the way it can in life. Of course the audience can leave the theater, but the play will still continue. For the time the audience sits before the performance of the play it shares time and space with the play.

These various kinds of separation, natural to the theater and imposed on it, could be taken advantage of to dramatize other more metaphysical kinds of separation that Wilder saw as defining the American. Most of these—the separation from time, place, tradition, and other Americans—I have already considered.

A distinction between the story—the story of George and Emily and their families and their town—and the idea or meaning is also important. The story of *Our Town* is banal, ordinary. I have already discussed the effects on the plotting: events are shown out of time sequence. They are without the usual sort of beginning and ending, but start and stop abruptly, often with an interruption from the Stage Manager. The separation between event and significance is a sort of meaning. What the characters understand from the events is the substance of the play.

Sol Lesser wished to change and augment both the story and the psychology of the characters when he was preparing the movie version.

> It has been suggested for movie purposes a means to be found to attach the third act to circumstances already within the play. . . . By this it is meant that perhaps there should be a problem affecting the married life of Emily and George growing out of the differences in their mentalities. I cite the following only as an example:—
>
> Emily is brighter than George; in her youth she has the best memory in her class—she recites like "silk off a spool"—she helps George in his mathematics—she is articulate—George is not—she is "going to make speeches all the rest of her life." . . .
>
> Query: Could it be Emily's subtlety in the soda-fountain scene that causes George to make the decision not to go to Agricultural School? The audience gets this, but George feels it is his own voluntary thought. He makes the decision not to go.
>
> Could Emily, after death, re-visit her fifth wedding anniversary . . . and now see her mistake?

Emily in life is likely to have been overambitious for George, wanting him to accomplish all the things he would have known had he gone to Agricultural School, but which he has had to learn mainly by experience. In a single sentence we could establish that George did not develop the farm as efficiently and as rapidly as Emily thought he should have. She continued to get ideas out of newspapers and books, as she did out of her school books, and had tried to explain them to George, but he was slow in grasping them. She had been impatient very often. Someone else's farm may have been progressing faster than George's and she may not have liked that. . . .

Now she sees this. She remembers she was responsible for his not going to Agricultural School. She has overlooked many of George's virtues—she took them all for granted. All this was her mistake. . . .

Could there be a great desire to live, to profit by what she has just seen, rather than go back to the grave—should she long to live—would the audience, witnessing this picture, pull for her to live—and she does?

Lesser wanted to supply the connections of plotting and motivation that would explain everything that Wilder had rejected. Lesser's interpretation of George and Emily's marriage would limit the idea of marriage to a particular, identifiable life. In other words, Human Nature. Lesser added, ". . . It would only change the expression of your philosophy, not the philosophy itself, which would be retained."[48] But the expression of Wilder's "philosophy" *is* the meaning.

Wilder, knowing exactly what he had accomplished on the stage, firmly resisted the suggested changes.

I feel pretty concrete about trying to dissuade you against showing Emily returning to her fifth wedding anniversary and regretting that she had been an unwise wife.

(1) It throws out the window the return to the 12th birthday which you feel is sufficiently [*sic?* insufficiently] tied up with the earlier part of the picture, but which is certain of its effect.

(2) It introduces a lot of plot preparation in the earlier part of the picture that would certainly be worse than what's there now. Scene of George running the farm incompetently. Scene of Emily upbraiding him.

(3) It makes Emily into a school-marm "improving" superior per-

son. The traits that you point out *are* in her character . . . but I put them there to prevent her being pure-village-girl-sweet-ingenue. But push them a few inches further and she becomes priggish.

(4) The balance of the play, reposing between vast stretches of time and suggestions of generalized multitudes of people requires that the fathers and mothers, especially the hero and heroine, be pretty near the norm of everybody, every boy and every girl.

If this is made into an ineffectual-but-good-hearted-husband and superior-interfering-wife, the balance is broken.

It's not so much new "plotting" that is needed, as it is refreshing detail-play over the simple but sufficient plot that's there.[49]

Wilder did not invent characters or a story that are interesting. They are "pretty near the norm of everybody." They have been liberated from identity of motivation, time, and place, where Lesser wanted to imprison them again. Anybody who criticizes *Our Town* for being a set of clichés is missing Wilder's intent. The play is full of clichés, but their significance, unlike the explanation Lesser offered, is not a cliché. Lesser's version is a hopelessly ordinary and dull anecdote.

Emily's "mistake" is not that she nagged George unfairly. Emily recognizes from the perspective of separation from the living how difficult and painful it is to know pure existing, to separate oneself from the supports of Human Nature, to live an intensely inner life.

Quite naturally, there is a separation in the language of *Our Town,* too; the separation of what is meant from what is said. Wilder wrote in his *Journals,* "Poetry is a language within the language that serves to describe de-individualized experience" (7). As this applies to *Our Town* it means that inside the language that presents heliotrope, strawberry phosphates, and hair ribbons, is another language, poetry. Inside the languages of the specific and particular is a language of the Human Mind.

Writing about the American language as part of his Charles Eliot Norton lectures at Harvard in 1950, Wilder addressed himself to two of its characteristics: "First, we observe that elevation and intensity are not solely and inseparably associated with noble images" (*AC,* 31–32). Loftiness and the sublime are available to Americans in a vocabulary of ordinary words from ordinary life. "Second, most European exercises in the sublime, in avoiding the common and the humble, avoid the specific" (*AC*, 32). Americans, on the other hand, are not satisfied with high vagueness. They demand a language that can encompass life's diversity: "The bigger the world is, the *less* you can be content with vagueness" (*AC*, 33).

Emily's blue hair ribbon, ordinary, trivial, and absurdly specific, is exactly the kind of language and image that Wilder describes. It is this hair ribbon that initiates the emotion too strong for her to sustain in her return and that triggers a rush of feeling in the audience, too. According to Wilder, images like the hair ribbon are *inclusive* because they are not amorphous. They do not distill truth. They isolate and fix value "on every existing thing in its relation to a totality, to the All, to the Everywhere, to the Always" (*AC*, 33). We may not all remember blue hair ribbons, but because the image is so exact, it allows all of us to believe that the one thing we do remember possesses a value analogous to the value we recognize in the play.

Wilder's use of ordinary language was deliberate and demanded selection and emphasis. He wrote of his struggle to find the right language for another play of his, *The Emporium*, "as always any stupidity comes from the fact that I have not found the common-common way of stating these things—*i.e.*, of feeling them validly in myself; for if they are not common common they are not good enough for me" (*J*, 51).

In eliminating traditional beauties like metaphor, unusual vocabulary, and elegant expression, Wilder also eliminated peculiarities of characterization and sophisticated ideas. The cost is great, and it disappoints or misleads many in the audience. But the rewards are great, too.

Some look for articulation of ideas in *Our Town,* and they look in vain. Some profess to find ideas spoken by characters, and they are comforted by the optimism or irritated by what they feel is the pseudoprofundity of what they find. They are all mistaken. Though the play does have ideas, they are dramatized, not voiced. Wilder wrote: "Works do not survive by reason of their ideas; with the exception of that minimal and infinitely gradual accretion of truly new ideas contained in the slow unfoldment of the religious interpretation of existence, all the ideas in the world have been here since recorded time; they are common knowledge; what are generally called ideas are transient observations on the transient conditions of society . . ." (*J*, 27–28). What most people think of as ideas are Human Nature, and they are eventually lost in time. True ideas are not new. Anybody knows them, so literature does not survive through its ideas. What then does make a work immortal?

"The virtue of prose," said Wilder, "lies in its movement." He used the Greek word *kinesis* for this motion in language: "It is *kinesis* which is the great glory of the King James Bible. That work has so long been surrounded with superstitious veneration that few have ventured to point out that throughout long stretches its ideas, in the temporal sense we indicated, are no longer valid, and that many of its most celebrated passages are meaningless." Though many people because of religious conviction would disagree with Wilder's evaluation of the Bible's glory and its out-of-date ideas, as a literary judgment his thought has validity. He repeated, "But books are not great by reason of the presence within them of their topical ideas, and many of the most treasured works of literature contain within them passages which are not today intelligible" (*J*, 28–29).

The language of plays has a peculiar kind of movement that is distinct from the movement of other prose. The source of movement in a play's language is the various kinds of separation. The strangest separation of all is like the unintelligible passages in "treasured works of literature." Many people have enjoyed plays presented in foreign languages they have either partly or completely not really understood. Shakespeare's language is only intermittently clear to most members of most audiences, yet the interested spectator derives pleasure from the plays in performance. And for some, the richness of the poetry is positively distracting from the theatrical experience. There is something both exhilarating and satisfying in the theater that has nothing to do with the rational discourse and ideas conveyed by the language. On a primitive level, there is the spectacle. I have shown how Wilder seized on stage surprises to keep his audience interested. But he knew these would not be surprising very long, that spectacle quickly becomes tiresome if it does not tell anything.

Wilder wanted to tell his audience that Americans exhibited this movement in a way different from others. Stein had written in *Lectures in America*,

> Something is always happening, anybody knows a quantity of stories of people's lives that are always happening, there are always plenty for the newspapers and there are always plenty in private life. Everybody knows so many stories and what is the use of telling

another story. What is the use of telling a story since there are so
many and everybody knows so many and tells so many. . . .

She did not want to tell stories of what was happening. Facts, events
are not interesting for themselves:

> So naturally what I wanted to do in my play was what everybody
> did not always know nor always tell. . . .
> I wanted still more to tell what could be told if one did not tell
> anything. . . .

She began writing plays that dramatized something new, something
apart from what could be told through ordinary intrigue. What was
it?

> I came to think that since each one is that one and that there are a
> number of them each one being that one, the only way to express
> this thing each one being that one and there being a number of them
> knowing each other was in a play. . . . And the idea . . . was to
> express this without telling what happened, in short to make a play
> the essence of what happened.[50]

Her idea was not something *about* living or an illustration of living,
but was living itself. It did not discuss ideas. A play was the best
expression of what she saw in living. What she saw is what Emily sees,
that everybody is an individual, unique and lonely, that there are lots
of individuals, and they know each other. What she saw was a universe full of separate beings. This is what Wilder dramatizes on stage:
Americans cannot derive any comfort or identity, any connection,
from anything outside of themselves, but they do recognize or assign
value to as much of all that otherness as they can.

The justification for emphasizing all of the separations that are
part of the theater is that they dramatize the separation that interests
Wilder in living. The first Americans' "sense of identity did not derive
from their relation to their environment. The meaning which their
lives had for them was inner and individual. . . . Independence is a
momentum. . . . separatism is a momentum" (*AC*, 10). The momentum is what Wilder called *kinesis* in his *Journals*. It is movement, and
Wilder's efforts to make his play move were at least partly the result

of making a language where "what it said [was separated] from what it did, what it was from what it held. . . ."[51] This is energy, and it is exciting. It is the characteristic Wilder recognizes in masterpieces. *Kinesis* is not to be confused with activity. The movement of *Our Town* is not the result of a lot of rushing around. It is an inner movement. Gertrude Stein noticed that the American soldiers standing around Paris after World War II were "filled with moving," although they were perfectly still. Her analogy was the motor of a car, which could run, even though the car itself was at rest.

Wilder's language for expressing the separation in the American experience is itself disconnected and disembodied. The characters do not say what Wilder means. They do not say his ideas. They say what they know, or as in the case of Mrs. Soames, what they do not know. And it is dramatic.

Wilder thought that, "It is the task of the dramatist so to coordinate his play, through the selection of episodes and speeches, that, though he is himself not visible, his point of view and his governing intention will impose themselves on the spectator's attention. . . ." The playwright is not directly visible, except as he appears in the play's ordered arrangement. Even there, he does not impose some reducible idea on the audience. He shows the audience what he knows, "not as dogmatic assertion or motto, but as self-evident truth and inevitable deduction" (*AC*, 125). This is a risky business. Most playwrights are so anxious about what the audience will think it sees and what it will deduce from the parts of the play, that they feel obligated to spell out what the audience should take home. And audiences expect such obvious lessons, so that where they do not appear, as in Shakespeare for example, the director usually supplies them through some distortion of the play. And in a play like *Our Town,* which is much more different from the usual theater fare than it seems, audiences will find ideas and prescriptions for living when they do not exist.

Though it is possible that Wilder might have wished to show pure existing disconnected from anything, he wanted even more for his play to succeed in the commercial theater. The character of the Stage Manager functions to make all the disconnections move one after another smoothly. Wilder said about the usual functions of such a character,

Many dramatists have regretted this absence of the narrator from the stage, with his point of view, his powers of analyzing the behavior of the characters, his ability to interfere and supply further facts about the past, about simultaneous actions not visible on the stage, and, above *all,* his function of pointing the moral and emphasizing the significance of the action. . . . But surely this absence constitutes an additional force to the form, as well as an additional tax upon the writer's skill.

(*AC,* 125)

The Stage Manager does analyze the characters, but only in general terms. "Strong minded people . . . come a long way to be independent" (80). "There's something way down deep that's eternal about every human being" (81). But what is it that is eternal? The Stage Manager never tells us. He interferes, sending actors offstage and summoning them on. He supplies facts: statistics, information about births and deaths. He informs the audience about what it will not see: Bryan's speech, for example, and the automobile. He even points the moral and emphasizes significance, often with a question: "Aren't they [the dead] waitin' for the eternal part in them to come out clear" (82). But he does not rob the events of their mystery as events taking place in front of us. There is no sense that he is telling us something that is already over and can be supplied with the perfect explanation. Wilder's dead are certainly waiting for the eternal part to come out. But it is not going to come out in any performance of the play as written. And furthermore it is not at all clear what it is that is the eternal part. Everybody in the audience is free to think of what that is for himself, if he needs to identify it. The Stage Manager's helpfulness in directly conveying ideas about the play's meaning is an illusion.

But his helpfulness as a character in the play is real enough. He interacts with the other characters in their roles both as actors and as inhabitants of Grover's Corners. He supplies information that the townspeople could not know: that the three acts of the play represent living, marriage, and death, though it is difficult to imagine anyone in the audience who could not figure that out for himself. Time of day, weather, and so on. Generalizations about life—mostly the sort any sensible adult knows already. But it is a serious error to mistake these truisms for some philosophy of life promoted by Wilder.

The effect of this activity is different from the information he provides. The Stage Manager repeatedly interrupts the illusion that the play is reality. He is vital to the play's structure in that he is the means for creating continuity between the wedding morning and the soda fountain scenes, for example. But even more significant is his act of calling attention to their disconnection in the sense of event. Though not, of course, in the way Wilder has constructed his plot. The Stage Manager makes it easier for the audience to accept what is strange in the play's presentation. But not because he eliminates the strangeness; his laconic manner is reassuring as he calls attention to what is strange.

Just as our lives move toward death, the "Great Event," so does *Our Town* build toward death in act 3. But it is not Emily's dying that is the subject of this act. We do not see her death, and its cause—childbirth—is mentioned only as a kind of representation of an ironic truth. Act 3 is a recognition of death. The entire act, which is a series of recognitions, is a developing recognition for the characters and audience.

In his introduction to Aristotle's *Poetics,* Francis Fergusson reminds us that "in good drama down to our own day such [recognition] scenes are essential. . . ."[52] Fergusson, like Aristotle, is writing of tragic effects, and *Our Town* is not a tragedy. But it is good drama, and like tragedy it manifests the "organic parts of drama": "Reversal of the Situation, Recognition, and Pathos."

"Reversal of the Situation," according to Aristotle, "is a change by which the action veers round to its opposite." And Francis Fergusson notes that "the objective situation does not change. . . . What changes is the situation as the thought of the characters makes it out at that moment."[53] What changes the situation is the perception of the situation by the characters. In *Our Town,* daily living stays the same. Emily's twelfth birthday morning is what it always was. But she perceives it differently, and it changes for her and perhaps even for some in the audience.

The excitement of such reversals is due to the fact that the reversal is what Emily recognizes. "The best form of recognition is coincident with a Reversal of the Situation."[54] Emily sees herself and lives her life, too, and she recognizes that her life was not what she thought it had been.

Wilder has presented for us Emily's entire being, not as it might be in real life clouded with complexity, but simplified and made clear as a character in a play. Emily's recognition, the reversal of what had seemed to be her life, produces the pathos. Emily sees her life more clearly, but she can do nothing about it. She is dead. She cannot live her life again, and she has no future life that she can change. As I have tried to show, the dead really dramatize a truth about the psyche of the living. What affects the audience in addition to Emily's plight is the recognition that they are really in the same boat. The earth is "too wonderful for anybody to realize."

The sturdiness of *Our Town* is the result of Wilder's playwriting skill. He employed the "organic parts" of drama so that the recognition scenes of act 3 build with certainty and accumulating effect.

The Stage Manager gradually reveals that the scene is the town cemetery. The cemetery is both part of the natural world in which it is set, and part of the human world because it began with the arrival of the European settlers. The cemetery is the perfect place to consider what is eternal in human beings. "And it ain't houses and it ain't names, and it ain't earth, and it ain't even the stars" (81). It is not in any sense material reality.

The dead are in the process of forgetting the material world. Memory goes. This loss of memory is inevitable and also painful. Much great writing since the beginning of the nineteenth century focuses on the examination of memory. Freud's work is perhaps the most obvious case, but Tennyson's *In Memoriam* is closer to Wilder's immediate subject because it connects loss of memory with the passing of time after the loss of a beloved. Marcel Proust, a favorite writer of Wilder, probes in great detail the new sorrow that is the result of the recognition that the original sorrow is fading. And Wilder like Proust is determined to discover what remains, though he was elated to replace Proust with the American Gertrude Stein and her idea of the Human Mind. Through the Stage Manager, the audience recognizes the place as the cemetery and they know what will be presented there.

The second recognition scene is between Joe Stoddard, who is arranging the funeral, and Sam Craig, who has returned, after being away, for the funeral. We learn that the funeral is for someone related to the Gibbses, who died in childbirth, that Mrs. Gibbs is dead, and that Simon Stimson committed suicide. The actors sitting in the chairs are gradually introduced as the dead. Although it is fairly certain, even for anyone who does not know the play, that the funeral is Emily's, tension rises as the audience waits for her appearance.

The third scene is introduced by the mourners carrying umbrellas. Whoever thought of the umbrellas—both Wilder and the producer-director Jed Harris are credited—they are an entirely successful, "spectacular" effect. They are black, melancholy, slightly grotesque and awkward, associated with superstition, and they portray man not very effectively trying to protect himself from nature. Emily appears from among the umbrellas in a white dress like the one for her wedding, and the audience recognizes her, at the same moment she recognizes the other dead.

Audience recognition of Emily is hardly the point, and there is so much more to acknowledge. Among the most important is that Emily does not like being new, and when she tells Mrs. Gibbs about the farm and does not get a very interested response, she realizes that she herself is no longer so interested in the affairs of the living as she thought she was. She begins to see that "Live people don't understand," and "how in the dark live persons are" (89–90), though she does not yet comprehend what this will mean to her.

Going back to "live all those days over again" (91) produces the big recognition: no one can look hard enough. But also that an effort to relive the past is not helpful. Wilder was delighted by Gertrude Stein's question: "What is the use of being a little boy if you are going to grow to be a man?" (*AC*, 189). What does the past mean? What is the purpose of living in time? The question, I suppose, is its own answer. Wilder (like Tennyson and Proust before him) dramatized the recognition that when sorrow for the beloved dead goes, its passing is indeed painful and a new sorrow takes its place ("I will remember you forever" is both humanly true in that the person speaking means it, and realistically false in that it is not possible). But the process of forgetting is also a comfort.

When George falls at Emily's feet while the dead talk of the stars, there is a final recognition of the one and the millions and millions. The Stage Manager can send the audience home.

Wilder's first full-length play, *The Trumpet Shall Sound*, was a kind of religious allegory. In the introduction to *The Angel That Troubled the Waters*, he wrote, "Almost all of the plays in this book are religious, but religious in that dilute fashion that is a believer's concession to a contemporary standard of good manners. . . . It is the kind of work I would most like to do well, in spite of the fact that there has seldom been an age when such a vein was less welcome and less understood."[55] At first Wilder identified the difficulty of writing a religious play with finding the right language: "The revival of religion is almost a matter of rhetoric."[56] Probably the experience of writing *The Bridge of San Luis Rey* and *The Woman of Andros* taught Wilder that there could be no new language without a new idea of religion. Again Wilder was fortunate because of his friendship with Gertrude Stein. In the introduction to *Four in America,* Wilder surveys Stein's ideas about religion in America. He acknowledges that the passages dealing with religion in her work are among the most difficult, because she had difficulty expressing her insight.

Basic to her use of the term religion is her distinction of the idea of religion from cults and dogma. This distinction helped Wilder to see that not only could religion exist apart from particular sects and their distinctive beliefs, but also that it could exist apart from the dominant religion of Western civilization, Christianity. Wilder explained, "Religion is what a person knows—knows beyond knowing, knows beyond anyone's power to teach him—about his relation to the existence in which he finds himself" (*AC,* 207–8).

Scattered throughout his *Journals,* Wilder wrote about religion, sometimes prompted by his reading, sometimes by problems he was confronting in his writing. In his distress while reading *Pierre* at having to deal with what he thought was Herman Melville's "ever-youthful surprise that there was evil in the universe," he turned to reading Leo Tolstoi's *War and Peace.* He felt that he and Tolstoi shared the problem of "not to dare too narrowly to define what I mean—what he means—by [a novel by a man who believes in God]" (*J,* 123). Wilder here was trying to discover a way to explain Tolstoi, but after some theorizing about the novel and Tolstoi's concept of God's nature, he considers the "consequences that flow from the God-interest of Tolstoi" (*J,* 125). These "consequences" sound remarkably like a description of the folks in Grover's Corners, and his explanation of Stein's religion. It hardly matters for our purposes that Wilder may have been using Tolstoi to objectify his own views: "From it [the God-interest] proceeds the absolutely equalized attention to the specific detail . . .: every person, every nation, every moment in time is unique . . .; each is himself in the God-relationship vertically, not in the community-relationship horizontally" (*J,* 125). Or, as Wilder put it about Stein, "Americans do not localize anything, not even themselves. . . . and a congregation of four hundred is not four hundred, but it is one and one and one and one . . . up to four hundred" (*AC,* 208). Stein's hypothetical saint, General Grant, "for relief or guidance or comfort or support . . . did not ally himself with anyone else" (*AC,* 211). Americans think of themselves as individuals, not as part of a group, and they do not localize anything. Every place is unique and universal, too.

Wilder calls the awareness of uniqueness in Tolstoi's characters "passionless power." It results from their inability to find a way to fulfillment in their relation to existence, just what Emily sees on her "return." And it is "terrifying," but "not because they are a petrified determinism but because they are potential—they could have been reached in the freedom accorded to human beings" (*J*, 125). Their error was not predetermined by character, or psychology, or environment, or fate. They might have achieved their desire.

Wilder wrote similarly about Stein's saint General Grant and his hypothetical alter ego, "They did not let will or determination order them about" (*AC*, 211). Human failure is not determined by anything outside themselves, and failure is not the last word. Even after death something continues to struggle to understand.

Wilder's conclusions about the failures of Tolstoi's characters is a description of the failure in seeing everything that pains Emily in act 3: "after the deaths of the Prince and Liza they [the living] continue, straining, bursting to reach their right due fulfillment. God's interest never flags: from Natasha's error (itself an expression of the passional life as a creativity) will come a glorious deepening of her union with Prince Andrey, just as he will have gained it from his error in his married life" (*J*, 125). Failure is a sign of living. Emily because she sees herself living, through what she sees as her inadequacy in living, grows to a greater understanding of herself. But since she has no ordinary life where it can be realized, she must return to the cemetery.

Wilder wrote about Stein's and Tolstoi's religion that the human creature saw himself in living in a specific and individual relationship with existence. This "existence" is what has traditionally been called God. Wilder asks, "And what is God's interest but that these . . . limited human beings find their God-relationship in the natural human life?" (*J*, 125). That thing that the Stage Manager calls "eternal" is to be discovered in living. But Wilder a little later is more specific: "And all these deaths [in *War and Peace*] charge the book with life, irradiate it—not . . . by making us prize more highly the sense-experience of living—but by making us prize the more highly the human relationships and depth one can put into them" (*J*, 126).

The God-relationship is found in "the natural human life," in human living. And it is not to make us more aware of physical living, not "sense experience." Awareness of the value of human relationships is the reward. The value is of our own making; we put it into the relationships. "Abstract! Abstract!" This is once more the contrast between Human Nature and the Human Mind.

Wilder wrote in his *Journals*, "Oh, the difficulty of establishing the Emporium [this was also the title of his unfinished play] as the Excellent, as Gertrude [Stein]'s Human Mind, and at the same time making it somehow fleetingly represent what centuries have called "God—as the Other" (*J*, 51).

The "delirious appreciation of each moment of consciousness" is what is eternal, is the Human Mind, is the God-relationship. The "dead" in *Our Town* are forgetting the "sense experience of living" and acquiring "passionless power." They are becoming the depth of what they gave to their relationship with others. But it is the relationship, not the other person, that survives. This is what Emily observes when she says that the living are blind. George in mourning Emily's death has forgotten the great gift of his relationship with her. Now we all know that this is entirely natural in life, but *Our Town* is a play. It is important and right for Wilder to present for the audience the idea that our anxiety about errors in living and the pain endured from the dying of those we love are a means to deepening our awareness. This is not to comfort those in mourning when they are enduring the real pain of their loss. It is simply to present a truth from the distance of timelessness. This can happen, the play says.

Wilder wrote that in American religion, "all you have is in every moment of your consciousness . . . and so self-contained is every moment of consciousness that there is nothing left over for expectation or memory. The American, then, who has lost that moment of consciousness is not that European thing called "dead"—so fraught with immemorial connotations—he has gone away" (*AC*, 210). The American lives in consciousness or knowing, and when he dies, there is no sense of personal survival in monuments or any other ways of fixing the memory. And there is no "expectation" either. Wilder's "dead" are not waiting for a paradise where their individual selves will be fulfilled. They are going away, "Waitin' for the eternal part in them to come out clear" (82). It is easier to see what the "eternal part" is not than it is to define it, except to say that it is perhaps something like the Human Mind floating free from sense experience.

The living, of course, fall short of this ideal perfection of the dead. This is Wilder's definition of "sin." He rejects the idea that sin is a failure to conform to current mores, or is mostly sexual, or "linked up with the Crucifixion—our 'murder'" (*J*, 10). Wilder found the Crucifixion a fine metaphor, but he rejected its actual "involvement in blood and murder" (*J*, 10). The blood-guilt prevented the spiritual values

from making themselves heard. Wilder found support for this idea in
G. B. Shaw, who also thought Christianity was unhealthily obsessed
with the blood of the Crucifixion, calling Christians, "Crosstians."

"The sense of having sinned," Wilder wrote, "[proceeds] from a
continuous and accelerating consciousness in man that he is falling
short of a series of perfection-requirements that were implanted in his
soul before birth and which came from the order of the universe . . ."
(J, 10). The sense of sin is awareness of error. It derives from consciousness, the Human Mind. It is knowing that one has not fulfilled
one's potential. And from what Wilder wrote about Tolstoi, we know
that the potential he had in mind was for depth of human relationship.
And also, from what he wrote of Andrey and Natasha, we know Wilder believed that consciousness of error does not lead to despair, but
to greater consciousness. The religious part of *Our Town* is not directed to pointing out human failure or to demanding that we amend
our lives, but to clarifying, however briefly, consciousness.

Wilder wrote that he was stimulated by his reading of Goethe to
identify the natural "sense of having sinned" with the norm in the
universe—"not the beasts of the field" (J, 10). He found in Goethe the
idea of "a stream of energy" pouring from the heart of the universe
that is "ceaselessly operative," molding "chaos into significant form
. . . urging on of the random and the incoherent toward meaningful
shape" (AC, 145). But just as in his observations about Stein and Tolstoi, he said, "The shapes toward which all things tend are not determined in advance" (AC, 145).

"This *Wirkende*—achieving force—is *ewig*—it will never come to
an end" (AC, 145). And it is generally benign. Sometimes "our Na-
ture-God glows with love, but the love which exists in Goethe's concept of nature is of another thought-world than that which is radical
in Christian doctrine" (AC, 146). With some energy Wilder rejected
the Christian identification of God with a loving father: "These unloving demanders-of-love are spoiled children who want in perpetuity
the being-loved condition of infancy, and the being-loved situation in
which American protestantism presented the cosmos. 'God is love;
God is father'—these phrases constituted a cosmic environment which
broke down" (J, 186).

The relation to the existence in which Wilder's religious American
finds himself is not some sentimental, or romantic, psychological notion of love, though it can be loving, and certainly it is not resenting,

despising or even trying to control or change. *Our Town* is not about not loving one another enough, but about looking at everything hard enough. Emily's words should be repeated: "I can't look at everything hard enough" (97).

An important corollary to the rejection of a caring, loving universe is the foolishness of wishing or trying to force circumstances to one's will. The unending achieving force wishes us well, but

> It does not hear our supplications. It does not grieve over our mistakes. The whole erring planet may go up in smoke, but the *ewig Wirkende* will continue gloriously, joyously, pressing chaos into new significant forms. . . . it is the All and it is eternal. . . . We cannot be sure that it will . . . connect with us, as we could wish. It is capricious. It does not necessarily reward our merits of hard work or our longing.
>
> (*AC*, 146)

These ideas of an upwardly spiraling activity in the universe can be found in G. B. Shaw, especially in *Back to Methuselah,* as well as in Goethe. The eternal in all of us that the Stage Manager says the dead are waiting for to come out clear is their participation in the creative force of the universe. The human feelings of grieving, rewarding, and punishing are foreign to it. Wilder wrote of Stein's religion, "The skies do not pity nor punish, nor bring gifts" (*AC*, 210).

Goethe's *ewig Wirkende* "does not hear our supplications," Stein's "American religion is thanking, not supplication" (*AC*, 208). Along with the immediate notions of sin, Wilder firmly thought the decline of the church was due to the emphasis "on prayer as a request for an interference with cause and effect" (*J*, 10). Stein's American does not ask God, or the Human Mind, or the *ewig Wirkende,* or God-in-nature to swerve from its path for his individual benefit, which would be either monumentally egocentric or silly or both at once. "It is at the very heart of American religion that the majority of Americans 'like what they have'" (*AC*, 208). The idea of prayer is to be so pleased with what is surrounding, that we neither despise it nor impose our will on it.

But Wilder's Americans are not passive. "The true passivity—that is the true slavery and the true ineffectiveness—is to wish and to wait and to yearn and to conspire" (*AC*, 209). The really passive kind of person either prays for something different or tries to change reality, either himself or his environment, through an act of will. Mrs. Webb and Mrs. Gibbs have "brought up two children apiece, washed, cleaned the house,—and *never a nervous breakdown*" (47). The two women have lived the lives they found themselves in. Wilder is not prescribing a life for all women. He is describing a narrow, essential life that was as full of productivity—effective action—as LIFE allowed. Mrs. Gibbs wanted to go to France, and though apparently Mr. Gibbs resisted her, she did not fret. She gave the money to George and Emily. Her failure to visit France is not sad. That she wanted to go is evidence of her awareness of life outside Grover's Corners, but not seeing France does not diminish her. She lived her life as she could. And she nags George even on his wedding morning to put on his overshoes because she knows wet feet can result in colds.

Mrs. Gibbs sings in a church choir and obviously participates in church services and hears protestant sermons, but her true religious life is in her daily living, apart from all theology, sects, and rituals. Her relationship with her family is her relationship with the eternal. And it is the relationship that participates in the eternal, not the family. The family is an accident of nature, and it will disappear in time.

There is no sense that anyone in *Our Town* is afraid of death. The characters do not feel themselves outside of nature. They are not fighting against it. The Stage Manager presents several views of the cemetery, each representing an attitude toward death. The cemetery is an important part of the town. One can see far in any direction from the cemetery on a fine afternoon. Death is necessary for the long view of life in Grover's Corners. The cemetery has been where it is since the beginning of the town. And some come to look at the tombstones and some come in search of ancestors. Both activities are described as harmless "nonsense," the first because it lacks perspective on present time, and the second because an antiquarian interest in the past—the dead—can only obstruct and interfere with present consciousness. There are Civil War veterans who had "never seen more than fifty miles of [the United States] themselves. All they knew was the name, friends—the United States of America. . . . And they went and died about it" (80–81). Here Wilder calls attention to his American's attachment to idea, but not to place. The soldiers did not die for a piece of ground but for an abstraction, the Union. The Stage Manager tells us about the grief of the living when they bring their dead to the cemetery, and then after time passes, grief dies and then so do we, and when we do, we will be buried in the cemetery, too. And then he concludes with the important idea that the dead are being weaned away from the earth, so the "eternal part in them [can] come out clear" (82).

Wilder does not know anything more about being dead than any of the rest of us. His play is not for the dead, and he makes no promises, unlike most writers who want to create a religious work, for our future when we living are dead. Whatever the dead really do, Wilder is describing a perfect condition against which his living, religious American measures his achievement. The dead embody "passionless power," energy that is not distracted by feelings for the ephemeral, seductive natural world. They are Human Mind free of Human Nature. They are pure God-relationship.

Wilder also knows that we are all surrounded by the seductive world of Human Nature. His greatest irony is that the world of Human Nature is the means to discover the Human Mind. "Natural human life" and "human relationships" are the life we all live, if we are lucky. And part of this irony is that our unhappiness when we fail at the "natural human life" and "human relationships" is the surest sign that we have born in us "from the order of the universe" a sense of that perfection the dead are slowly acquiring.

Emily had a good life, growing and being a wife to George. That is why it is painful to return; it was good enough to make her aware how it fell short, and also good enough for her to leave it. She cannot change it. She can only see it.

Wilder is not counseling a retreat from the world like some cartoon Oriental swami meditating on a peak in the Himalayas. Living, making mistakes, being ceaselessly active until the end are necessary to find the God-relationship. Wilder said about Tolstoi: "the more a thing is *natural* the more it is *supernatural*" (*J*, 125). This is not mystical or ecclesiastical. It is simply a demand that we turn our attention to what is basic. We are all surrounded, but "'Surround does not mean surrender' [which] is . . . the loss of one's knowing" (*AC*, 211). The ideal is to know what we know "at the moment of knowing it," to be free of intention and expectation. The characters in *Our Town* in their living "did what they did, but they did not set about to do what they were to do" (*AC*, 211). And also "Americans do not wait—that is, they do not live in the expectation that circumstance is coming toward them bearing gifts" (*AC*, 210).

Writing about Emerson, Wilder described the paradox of what he saw in American independence from the social group, environment, and organized religion. Emerson, he says,

> was—to use a much admired phrase—sufficient to himself. And here we are back to our American individualism. That's what American individualism is: sufficiency to oneself. That Americans are also lonely and hence *in*sufficient to themselves is only apparently a contradiction: for they are sufficient to themselves without being able to make that sufficiency into a sufficiency to the whole experience of life which includes themselves.
>
> (*J*, 154)

Our Town is about Wilder's American being sufficient to himself but including at the same time an acknowledgment of as much of the total experience to which he is not sufficient as he can. "Americans cannot . . . be a success. . . . Americans are really only happy when they are failures" (*AC*, 209). Wilder wrote that these statements should not be interpreted sentimentally or in moralizing terms. "Moralizing comes from that realm of belief which is acquired, learned, arrogated to oneself and promulgated; but which is not truly believed or lived by" (*AC*, 209). Wilder is not moralizing in *Our Town*, as so many playgoers either wish or imagine he is. He is dramatizing what he sees in the American Mind, and of course, in his own as well. Americans are happy when they are failures because then they are most intensely alive and knowing what they know. Being a failure is exhilarating because it means that there is still a need to live. Being a failure is being unfinished, is recognizing that there is still more. When Emily tells George about the perfection of fathers, she is expressing an ideal that both she and George cannot reach, but both the ideal and her failure are real to her. Both are what Wilder dramatizes when she returns for her twelfth birthday.

7

On Stage

By its very nature the mounting of a play in production, especially a new play, always involves surprising excitements. Partly because Wilder was inexperienced with Broadway production, but also partly because of aspects of the situation apart from Wilder, the events created by bringing *Our Town* to New York seem particularly difficult. Some of them bring into relief aspects of the play.

Jed Harris is almost always described as a brilliant director. His production record was exceptional, both with classical revivals and Broadway entertainments, and many on both sides of the footlights speak eloquently of his theatrical imagination. But Harris was also difficult. Laurence Olivier, for example, who had been directed by Harris, claimed later that he had based his performance of Shakespeare's grotesque villain Richard III on Harris. Although Harris and Wilder had been briefly together at Yale, and Harris was the father of Wilder's close friend Ruth Gordon's child, Wilder did not know him well. Harris saw a draft of *Our Town*, as promised by Wilder, while both men were in Europe. Harris apparently regarded *Our Town* as his opportunity to have his hand in the creation of an original American masterpiece, an accomplishment so far missing from his list. He proclaimed, no doubt in part for the publicity value and also to encourage the actors, that *Our Town* was a "certain classic" and "that it might very well be the best American play ever written."[57] His enthusiasm for the play swept Wilder along and back to New York for rewriting and plans for production.

Harris believed in the overwhelming importance of casting. He selected Frank Craven, who came out of retirement, for the crucial role of the Stage Manager. The choice was made without consulting Wilder, who was understandably not entirely pleased with Harris's highhanded ways. Casting Emily also had problems. Martha Scott, who gave what was probably the performance of her life in the role, was the third actress selected for the role, and only eight days before the scheduled premiere out-of-town at Princeton's McCarter Theatre. Both actors were to set their mark on these roles, but for a new playwright these difficulties were upsetting.

Harris began rehearsals by warning the actors against any sentimentality in their playing, insisting that the key to the play was "dryness." Wilder certainly agreed, adding that "nostalgia" had to be eliminated. Sentimentality, of course, has been characteristic of many bad productions of *Our Town*, but has also been the source of much pleasure for those whose only contact with theater is in school and other amateur productions. But Harris clearly understood the style of the play and the greatest danger to that style.

Wilder's anxiety about false feeling in the performance of the actors was not entirely allayed by rehearsals. Edward P. Goodnow, who was the play's literal stage manager, recalled that at the first complete run-through of the play Wilder berated Harris for Frank Craven's sentimental performance. Harris expressed patience with Wilder's ignorance of rehearsal procedure, although apparently with little effect on Wilder's unhappiness. Before asking the company to do the whole play again, Harris praised the actors and whispered something briefly to Craven. Goodnow says that Wilder after the second run-through was as excited as he had been after the first, but now because Craven was "so rare and dry and fine." What had Harris whispered to Craven? "All I said was, Frank, I think this time you might put away your cello."[58]

Harris understood also that the audience would need some times in the play to respond to feeling from the acting. Goodnow recorded that he told Martha Scott that Emily's "Good-bye, World" speech was like a great aria in an opera. He said that "the actress who played 'Emily' could consider herself a failure if she did not get at least one letter a day from some play-goer, telling her how much more meaningful each passing moment of life had become."[59] The emphasis on the importance of feeling in this speech had a grotesque element. Rosamond Pinchot, who was in charge of props, committed suicide before the opening in New York. At least one newspaper suggested a causal connection between *Our Town*'s theme and her unhappy death. Martha Scott recalled that the cast had been told that one of Miss Pinchot's suicide notes had included Emily's farewell speech. Harris is reported to have deliberately used the death during rehearsal for acting motivation. Whether the exploitation of Miss Pinchot's death was heartless or not, it does point up the universal feeling in Wilder's language.

The language was to be one of the enduring sources of disagreement between Wilder and Harris. On the positive side of the collaboration, Wilder has acknowledged that Harris's advice about cuts in the text was good. Harris suggested that a scene concerning Emily and George's first meeting was a necessary element in the play, thereby provoking Wilder to write the soda fountain scene. Harris was possibly responsible for the very moving use of umbrellas at the grave site in act 3. He devised the effective lighting to indicate mood and place. These were all invaluable contributions.

But Harris also encouraged the actors to improvise their speeches, and he added speeches of his own. At one point he even suggested— and Wilder was not the only playwright to whom Harris made this demand—that he be considered coauthor. It was probably this action that lead Wilder to complain to Harris after the first performance, as the actor, José Ferrer reports, "You know, you've never understood that one scene, the dead at the end."[60] Or more sweepingly, as Goodnow wrote, "You simply do not understand my play!"[61] Or perhaps more to the point, "You've spoiled my shining prose."[62]

José Ferrer remembered his response to the premiere performance: "Thornton's achievement, so much of it, was Harris's. A playwright doesn't cast. . . . Lighting is not a playwright's doing and in this production there *was* scenery: the lighting was scenery."[63]

Wilder's melodramatic and pretentious characterization of his "shining prose" particularly irritated Harris. His answer, "Prose doesn't play,"[64] reveals the difference between the two men and I suppose the eternal and proper difference between a serious playwright and the director of a particular production. Wilder's ambition, though it included theatrical necessity, was also literary. He had written a play that he hoped would endure beyond the success of the original production in 1938. Harris's concern was quite properly to ensure the immediate theatrical success of his production. José Ferrer testified eloquently to Harris's achievement with casting and lighting and so on, and as a career man of the theater quite naturally he was struck by the theatricality of the production. Theatrical success makes money and creates reputation and fame, but it is eventually lost in the past.

In his *Journals,* Wilder acknowledged to himself the use in *Our Town* of lighting effects, and he set himself to find a means in his next play to deny himself the help of lighting to create an imagined scene (*J,* 43). He also wrote to Gertrude Stein that he recognized Harris's suggestions about structure were often good, but that he was always wrong about the words. His hope was eventually—and finally in the printed text—to eliminate all Harris's additions and interpolations.

Our Town was scheduled to play in Boston for two weeks after the premiere in Princeton. At Princeton it received unenthusiastic notices, and in Boston the situation was even worse. Because the play was losing money, Harris considered closing it before New York. But Marc Connelly, the author of *Green Pastures,* went to see *Our Town* in Boston and thought it would be successful. Perhaps his view was predetermined by his investment in the production. Alexander Woolcott, the *New Yorker* columnist, also went to Boston and agreed with Connelly. His opinion was important because of his influential ability to create publicity.

Later Harris apparently had an all but guaranteed good notice from another reviewer, Brooks Atkinson of the *New York Times.* His review mattered only slightly less than the *Times* reviews do today. There are several versions of how it came about and what the motives of Harris and Atkinson were, but in all of them Atkinson accepted an invitation from Harris to watch a run-through of a rehearsal. He was concealed in the balcony, and the performers were not informed of his presence. Like most of *Our Town*'s audience, he was moved by the play, especially the third act. His response was favorable, and furthermore he would not have to deal immediately with the strangeness of the play's experimental production in a matter of an hour or so while he wrote his review. He would come to the New York opening prepared.

Harris still did not have a New York theater, and the disarray in Boston was making theater owners back away. He took a risk and persuaded Gilbert Miller to let him have the Henry Miller Theatre for a single night (by chance, he got another week) and for nothing. Closing in Boston before the scheduled run was over, he opened early in New York, hoping for a success and another house being made available for a long run. It all worked as Harris had expected. Perhaps ignorant of Harris's incredible maneuvering, but certainly wanting to emphasize the experimental nature of his play and maybe even express his own anxiety, Wilder wrote later that the producer of *Our Town* had had so little faith in it that he had booked it for only one night in New York. Wilder's statement certainly makes *Our Town*'s success look even more exceptional, but Harris never doubted the worth of the play, and he understandably was angered by Wilder's comment.

The opening of *Our Town* along with its other difficulties was true to the theatrical myth in which the leading actor becomes ill on opening night but the show goes on. The actress who was playing Mrs. Gibbs, Evelyn Varden, collapsed in her dressing room with a fever, but galvanized by the tradition of the gallant trouper and helped by a shove from Harris, she entered on cue and carried on her performance. That the company's stage manager had broken his shoulder that afternoon was a minor problem.

There was off-stage drama related to the nature of *Our Town* that was played between Harris and the stagehands' union. The union objected to the absence of scenery and was totally opposed to actors moving the props. They regarded it as a ploy to avoid having to hire any stagehands. Harris finally agreed to employ half a dozen stagehands, but demanded that they not touch a single chair. The stagehands insisted upon doing what they regarded as their work. At curtain time no agreement had been reached with them. There are several accounts of what took place, each differing in detail, but all agree that there was a physical confrontation between Harris and at least one stagehand. He threatened with a fire-axe any stagehand who touched a chair and shoved the leader of the union down a flight of stairs. When two of the property men still insisted on handling chairs, Harris bombarded them with a stream of colorful invective, punched one of them to the floor and choked the other "into insensibility."[65] With no further trouble from the stagehands, the opening performance in New York went smoothly.

Though the final words were greeted with silence from the audience, when the curtain was raised for the cast to take its bows, they were greeted with enthusiastic cheers. Glenway Wescott, the American writer, recalled meeting Wilder at the stage door after the curtain on opening night. Wilder was uneasy, nervous about the play's success, trembling. Wescott tried to reassure him with praise for the play's originality and power, confessing that the fears of George and Emily in the wedding scene had brought tears to his eyes. "Fine! fine!" Wilder exclaimed, "if you don't mind shedding tears. Most men do mind, nowadays, I'm afraid. Even some women mind!" In a calmer moment later Wilder wrote with some humor that the tears shed at act 3 would be a helpful cure for a cold.

Wescott remembered that he also told Wilder, who obviously had not believed one word of it, that perhaps the play was too delicate, too philosophical, too sad to be a great box-office success. Wilder was right not to believe Wescott; the play has been successful everywhere in the world except, as Wescott notes, in France and England.[66]

Recently the fiftieth anniversary of the premiere of *Our Town* was observed. The Long Wharf Theater in New Haven, Connecticut—where Wilder went to Yale (he also lived nearby for many years) combined the city's 350th anniversary with that of *Our Town* in a production of the play. A new musical version called *Grover's Corners,* which probably would not have pleased Wilder, toured the country.

There have been at least two other musicals; neither was successful. One of them starred Frank Sinatra on television. Wilder especially disliked it, though he was happy to have the money it paid. Aaron Copland, the American composer whose music Wilder admired and who wrote the score for the movie version, wanted to score *Our Town* as an opera, but Wilder refused permission. He probably felt the play was just fine as it was and did not need any music.

Several important revivals, of course, have taken place since 1938. One of those important to Wilder was at Circle in the Square; it was part of the close relationship between that theater company and Wilder toward the end of his life. Several of his one-act plays were premiered there. But generally Wilder did not like the revivals. Perhaps the time was not right for them.

Mel Gussow, the *New York Times* critic, wrote about the fiftieth anniversary of the play that "*Our Town* may be the most misunderstood and misinterpreted of American plays. It is not a hymn to small town life. . . . Nor is it . . . a poetic memory piece." Gussow also reminds his readers that "stylistically and thematically, *Our Town* was, *and is* [emphasis added], a pioneering work of experimental theater . . . the play challenged traditions of stage time, characterization and scenic design."[67] He suggests that *Our Town* is alive and well on the American stage today and that it lives in the work of some of the best contemporary American playwrights, including Lanford Wilson, Sam Shepard, and David Mamet "in terms of finding the extraordinary within the most ordinary situations." Wilder would like that. He enjoyed the young and the new. "I should be very happy," he wrote in the Preface to *Our Town,* "if, in the future, some author should feel indebted to any work of mine. Literature has always more resembled a torch race than a furious dispute among heirs" (xiii). Lanford Wilson wrote on the same page as Gussow with a comic "straight face," "I didn't think I had been influenced by *Our Town.* . . . Some of Wilder's stage tricks, yes, but not really by *Our Town.* I was shocked when I reread the play. The Stage Manager's opening speech was completely stolen from Matt's first speech in my play *Talley's Folly,* I could see. And it was totally unconscious. That's being influenced."[68]

A very unusual manifestation of *Our Town* was as part of the Wooster Group's performance piece, *The Road to Immortality—Part One (Route 1 & 9).* It was first performed in 1981 and revived in 1987, both times controversially, though not because of its use of Wilder's play.

Our Town shows up first indirectly in a parody of Clifton Fadiman delivering an *Encyclopedia Brittanica* lecture on the meaning of the play in a film strip that is played on television monitors. It is awkward, with sound distortion, and clearly shows its age. The scenes from *Our Town* are full of heavy music and close-ups of the actors' faces, all of it inappropriate. The tone is pedantic and condescending, and it is clearly directed to a high school audience.

Scenes from *Our Town* are played on the monitors, too, not as part of the lecture, but in the general style of television soap opera. At the same time white actors in blackface (this was the source of the controversy) are performing a routine of the black vaudeville comedian Pigmeat Markham and generally mirroring the action of *Our Town* in the guise of black ghetto life, as well. Often the action was crude, sometimes sexual, sometimes overt, sometimes furtive. The first impression was that the two—*Our Town* and the blackface drama— were antithetical, but it did not quite work out that way when I saw it.

The audience reacted to the *Encyclopedia Brittanica* film strip with laughter because it *was* ridiculous. When the scenes from *Our Town* began, there was snickering at first, but gradually it stopped. The audience clearly found itself compelled by the performance of the bits of the play on the monitors. The style was totally inappropriate. Elizabeth LeCompte, one of the creators of *The Road to Immortality,* said, "I realized that when you took the Stage Manager out of *Our Town*, it became soap opera."[69] This remark is only partly true. Wilder's language and construction create meaning, too. But the audience was not watching *Our Town* just because flickering televisions or soap operas are tyrannical attention-getters. The audience plainly was interested in *Our Town*, and this was a sophisticated group out for an evening with one of the most up-to-date avant-garde performance groups. One of the performers, Peyton Smith, became aware that audiences directed their attention more to the monitors than to the live actors. Her explanation was that the audience was embarrassed by the activities on the stage, thinking, "I'm just going to stare up there. I don't want to be a voyeur."[70] The real explanation the night I saw the performance is that *Our Town* is better than what was happening on the stage floor. Here was an extreme case of a performance of *Our Town* being beyond the control of Wilder, but he had organized "the play in such a way that its strength survived" (*AC*, 117). *Our Town* is a sturdy play.

Even Elizabeth LeCompte admitted to her irritation at liking the filmed bits. It made her angry; she "couldn't go with it," but she could not destroy it either.[71] She acknowledged that she was fighting the same battle against realism that Wilder had fought—that Wilder is her "predecessor," and that her piece "has its roots in Wilder's own intentions."[72]

David Savran, in his book *The Wooster Group, 1975–1985: Breaking the Rules,* wrote: "Ironically, during a period of retrenchment in the 1980s, in the midst of a revival of realistic playwrighting, Wilder's hope [that he had helped to prepare the way for a new drama] has been fulfilled less conspicuously by new dramaturgy than new performance, and most powerfully perhaps by a work that uses his own script as a starting point."[73]

Our Town is as new as this morning. A new performance, true to Wilder's intention, is still well in advance of the audience, and most every new play, too. We still have not caught up with this play that paradoxically can seem too familiar.

Our Town has a reputation for being sentimental. Certainly it has been played sentimentally with false emotion and nostalgia. The play is, without the help of theatrical tricks, emotionally powerful, and audiences are moved often to weep. I suspect that the sentimentality is in the audience. Mel Gussow, writing about a recent revival, said about Emily's pleading with the Stage Manager after she decides to leave the living and join the dead: "The moment may prove almost too strong and too memorable. Watching the play we all return to Our Towns." Audiences may be annoyed to discover that they are moved by what they want to believe they have rejected and left behind: the ordinary event of everyday living. They do not like to think of themselves weeping in the theater. Their irritation with themselves is transferred to the play, and they blame it for false poetry and for vulgar atmosphere and for cheap emotionalism.

Lanford Wilson wrote that "*Our Town* is a deadly cynical and acidly accurate play." This seems perhaps too strong rhetorically, and even he felt the need to apologize for the alliteration. But he is right to call attention to all the unhappy events in the play. By the play's conclusion almost everybody ends up dead, and one character is a suicide. The view of marriage is horrifying. And the heroine concludes that living human beings are blind to their own lives. "*Our Town* is," Wilson says, "hard as nails."

Gussow, though he warns that "One should not carry the comparison too far," observed, "Though certainly less mordant there is a kind of Beckett-like aspect in the author's intention. In *Our Town*, as in *Waiting for Godot,* one is born astride the grave." It is true that Wilder wants to keep before the audience an awareness of the inevitability of death. The point of the pastness of Grover's Corners is that it is past. Neither it nor its values can be or should be revived. Its very power is that it is gone forever and that we will in time be gone with it. But Wilder's view of death is not frightening. Death is a fact. To deny it is sentimental. To falsify it with illusions is sentimental. As a fact it forces Wilder to confront the painful awareness of living. Painful not because being alive is not enough, but because it is more than most humanity can accommodate.

What "the people a thousand years from now" will know about "the way we were: in our growing up and in our marrying and in our living and in our dying" is that the people of Grover's Corners did things as they found them. Their heroism is that they did what was before them; and did not waste time or energy wishing for something else. Their failure is that they lived knowing so little of what they were about.

If the audience leaves the theater exhilarated and not depressed by what they have witnessed, it is because *Our Town* has given them the sense, not of how they have fallen short, but of how much more they can do.

Notes

1. Michael Gold, "Wilder: Prophet of the Genteel Christ," *New Republic*, 22 October 1930, 266–67.

2. Brooks Atkinson, "Our Town," *New York Times*, 5 February 1938, 18.

3. Joseph Wood Krutch, "Drama," *Nation*, 19 February 1938, 224–25.

4. Quoted in Linda Simon, *Thornton Wilder: His World* (Garden City, N.Y.: Doubleday, 1979), 144.

5. Stark Young, "Place and Time," *New Republic*, 23 February 1938, 74.

6. Mary McCarthy, *Sights & Spectacles* (New York: Farrar, Straus & Cudahy, 1956), 27.

7. Ibid., x.

8. John Gassner and Bernard F. Dukore, *A Treasury of the Theatre*, vol. 2, 4th ed. (New York: Simon & Schuster, 1970), 835.

9. Gilbert A. Harrison, *The Enthusiast: A Life of Thornton Wilder* (New Haven: Ticknor & Fields, 1983), 187–88.

10. Ibid., 188.

11. Raymond Massey, *One Hundred Different Lives* (Boston: Little, Brown, 1979), 299.

12. Helmut Papajewski, *Thornton Wilder*, trans. John Conway (New York: Frederick Ungar, 1968), 108.

13. "Afternoon," *New Yorker*, 23 May 1959, 35.

14. Rex Burbank, *Thornton Wilder* (New York: Twayne, 1961), 96.

15. Malcolm Goldstein, *The Art of Thornton Wilder* (Lincoln: University of Nebraska Press, 1965), 107.

16. Francis Fergusson, "Three Allegorists: Brecht, Wilder, and Eliot," *The Human Image in Dramatic Literature* (Garden City, N.Y.: Doubleday Anchor, 1957), 60.

17. Robert Corrigan, *The Modern Theatre* (New York: MacMillan, 1964), 1075.

18. Donald Gallup, ed., *The Flowers of Friendship* (New York: Alfred A. Knopf, 1953), 305.

19. The quotations from Jarry are my translations from: Alfred Jarry, *Oeuvres complètes*, vol. 4 (Lausanne), 159–67.

20. James Joyce, *A Portrait of the Artist as a Young Man* (New York: Viking, 1964), 15–16.

21. Gertrude Stein, *The Making of Americans* (New York: Harcourt, Brace, 1934), 211.

22. George Bernard Shaw, "Man and Superman," *The Bodley Head Bernard Shaw*, vol. 2 (London: Bodley Head, 1971), 652.

23. Ibid., 728.

24. Ibid., 715.

25. Ibid., 668.

26. Ibid., 729.

27. Ibid., 662.

28. Stark Young, "Mei Lan-fang," *New Republic*, 5 March 1930, 270.

29. Thornton Wilder, "A Preface for *Our Town*," *New York Times*, 13 February 1938, sec. 2, p. 1.

30. Young, "Mei Lan-fang," 75.

31. Richard Boleslavsky, *Acting, the First Six Lessons* (New York: Theatre Arts Books, 1933, 1949), 107–8.

32. Gertrude Stein, *Narration* (Chicago: University of Chicago Press, 1935), 61.

33. Boleslavsky, *Acting, the First Six Lessons*, 88.

34. Ibid., 92.

35. Ibid.

36. "*Our Town*—From Stage to Screen," *Theatre Arts*, November 1940, 815.

37. Ibid., 824.

38. Gallup, ed., *The Flowers of Friendship*, 305.

39. Shaw, "Man and Superman," 669.

40. Stein, *Narration*, 18.

41. Ibid., 22.

42. Ibid., 18.

43. "*Our Town*—From Stage to Screen," 816.

44. Thornton Wilder, *The Angel That Troubled the Waters* (New York: Coward-McCann, 1928), 35.

45. Francis Fergusson, *Dante's Drama of the Mind* (Princeton, N.J.: Princeton University Press, 1953), 6–7.

46. Ibid., 14.

47. "*Our Town*—From Stage to Screen," 824.

48. Ibid., 817f.

49. Ibid., 818.

50. Gertrude Stein, *Lectures in America* (New York: Random House, 1935), 118f.

51. Ibid., 53.

52. S. H. Butcher, trans., *Aristotle's Poetics,* introduction by Francis Fergusson (New York: Hill and Wang, 1961), 17–18.

53. Ibid., 16–17.

54. Ibid., 72.

55. *The Angel That Troubled the Waters,* xv.

56. Ibid., xvi.

57. Martin Gottfried, *Jed Harris: The Curse of Genius* (Boston: Little Brown, 1984), 165.

58. Jed Harris, *Watchman, What of the Night?* (Garden City, N.Y.: Doubleday, 1963), 149.

59. Ibid., 146.

60. Gottfried, *Jed Harris,* 169.

61. Harris, *Watchman, What of the Night?,* 149.

62. Gottfried, *Jed Harris,* 169.

63. Ibid.

64. Harrison, *The Enthusiast: A Life of Thornton Wilder,* 183.

65. Ibid., 184.

66. Glenway Wescott, *Images of Truth* (New York: Harper & Row, 1964), 302–5.

67. Mel Gussow, "A Theatrical Vision Endures," *New York Times,* 20 December 1987, sec. 2, p. 36.

68. Lanford Wilson, "*Our Town* and Our Towns," *New York Times,* 20 December 1987, sec. 2, p. 36.

69. David Savran, *The Wooster Group, 1975–1985: Breaking the Rules* (Ann Arbor, Mich.: UMI Research Press, 1986), 32.

70. Ibid., 34.

71. Ibid., 17.

72. Ibid., 18.

73. Ibid.

Selected Bibliography

Primary Sources

Our Town is published in *Three Plays: Our Town, The Skin of Our Teeth, The Matchmaker.* An acting version is published by Samuel French. All of Wilder's important articles and introductions have been collected in *American Characteristics and Other Essays.*

Plays, Novels, and Stories

Alcestiad, or A Life in the Sun. New York: Harper & Row, 1978.

The Angel That Troubled the Waters and Other Plays. New York: Coward-McCann, 1928.

The Bridge of San Luis Rey. New York: A. & C. Boni, 1927.

The Cabala. New York: A. & C. Boni, 1926.

"Childhood." *Atlantic Monthly,* November 1960, 78–84.

The Eighth Day. New York: Harper & Row, 1967.

Heaven's My Destination. New York: Harper & Bros., 1935.

The Ides of March. New York: Harper & Bros., 1948.

The Long Christmas Dinner and Other Plays in One Act. New Haven, Conn.: Yale University Press, 1931.

The Matchmaker. Revision of *The Merchant of Yonkers.* New York: Harper, 1955.

The Merchant of Yonkers. New York: Harper & Bros., 1939.

Our Century. New York: The Century Association, 1947.

The Skin of Our Teeth. New York: Harper, 1942.

Theophilus North. New York: Harper & Row, 1973.

Three Plays: Our Town, The Skin of Our Teeth, The Matchmaker. New York: Harper & Bros., 1957.

The Trumpet Shall Sound. Yale Literary Magazine, act 1, October 1919, pp. 9–26; act 2, November 1919, pp. 78–92; act 3, December 1919, pp. 128–46; act 4, January 1920, pp. 192–207.

The Woman of Andros. New York: A. & C. Boni, 1930.

Nonfiction

American Characteristics and Other Essays. Edited by Donald Gallup. New York: Harper & Row, 1979.

The Journals of Thornton Wilder: 1938–1961. Edited by Donald Gallup. New Haven, Conn.: Yale University Press, 1985.

Translation

Lucrece, by André Obey. Boston: Houghton Mifflin, 1933.

Letters

The Flowers of Friendship: Letters Written to Gertrude Stein. Edited by Donald Gallup. New York: Knopf, 1953. Contains five letters from Wilder to Stein and Alice B. Toklas: pp. 303–7, 336–37, 338–39.

"*Our Town*—From Stage to Screen." *Theatre Arts,* November 1940, 815–24. Correspondence between Wilder and Sol Lesser about the movie production of *Our Town.*

Secondary Sources

Biography

Goldstone, Richard H. *Thornton Wilder: An Intimate Portrait.* New York: Saturday Review Press/E. P. Dutton, 1975.

Harrison, Gilbert A. *The Enthusiast: A Life of Thornton Wilder.* New Haven: Ticknor & Fields, 1983.

Simon, Linda. *Thornton Wilder: His World.* Garden City, N.Y.: Doubleday, 1979.

Critical Studies

Bryer, Jackson R. "Thornton Wilder and the Reviewers." *Papers of the Bibliographical Society of America,* 58 (1964): 34–49.

Burbank, Rex. *Thornton Wilder.* New York: Twayne, 1961.

Corrigan, Robert W. "Thornton Wilder and the Tragic Sense of Life." In *The Theatre in Search of a Fix,* 239–46. New York: Delacorte, 1973.

Edelstein, J. M. *A Bibliographical Checklist of the Writings of Thornton Wilder.* New Haven: Yale University Press, 1959.

Fergusson, Francis. "Three Allegorists: Brecht, Wilder and Eliot." In *The Human Image in Dramatic Literature,* 41–71. New York: Doubleday Anchor, 1957.

Goldstein, Malcolm. *The Art of Thornton Wilder.* Lincoln: University of Nebraska Press, 1965.

Goldstone, Richard. "Thornton Wilder." In *Writers at Work,* 99–118. Edited by Malcolm Cowley. New York: Viking, 1959.

Haberman, Donald. *The Plays of Thornton Wilder: A Critical Study.* Middletown, Conn.: Wesleyan University Press, 1967.

Harris, Jed. *Watchman, What of the Night?* New York: Doubleday, 1963.

Kosok, Heinz. "Thornton Wilder: A Bibliography of Criticism." In *Twentieth Century Literature* 9 (1963). 93–100.

Krutch, Joseph Wood. *The American Drama Since 1918.* New York: Braziller, 1957.

Kuner, Mildred C[hristophe]. *Thornton Wilder; the Bright and the Dark.* New York: Crowell, 1972.

Papajewski, Helmut. *Thornton Wilder.* Translated by John Conway. New York: Ungar, 1968.

Parmenter, Ross. "Novelist into Playwright." *Saturday Review of Literature,* 11 June 1938, 10–11.

Scott, Winfield Townley. "'Our Town' and the Golden Veil." *Virginia Quarterly Review* (January 1953):103–17. (Also appears in *Exiles and Fabrications,* New York: Doubleday, 1961.)

Stresau, Herman. *Thornton Wilder.* New York: Ungar, 1963.

Wescott, Glenway. *Images of Truth.* New York: Harper & Row, 1962.

Index

Index

About the Author

When he was a graduate student at Yale, Donald Haberman first met Thornton Wilder and his sister Isabel Wilder. He owes a great debt to their interest and generosity. Haberman is a professor of English at Arizona State University, where his areas of special interest are drama and modern British literature. The author of *The Plays of Thornton Wilder: A Critical Study* (1968) and *G. B. Shaw: An Annotated Bibliography of Writings about Him,* vol. 3 (1986) and coauthor of vol. 2 (1988), he has also written articles on Ford Madox Ford, Marcel Proust, Stéphane Mallarmé, James Joyce, Plautus, and Evelyn Waugh.